INSPIRE
CONSULT
SELL

Master the consultative communication skills of the best ***dental teams*** to deliver a world class patient experience.

JUSTIN LEIGH

Carly,
Sorry it's taken so long to get your copy. I hope it's worth the wait.
All the best,
Justin
x

Self-Published by Justin Leigh and Focus4growth Ltd.

ISBN Paperback - 978-1-912713-45-5

ISBN eBook - 978-1-912713-46-2

Table of Contents

Introduction

If you're practising in dentistry and you're speaking with patients about treatment options and solutions or you're leading a team that does then, this is a book that will help you. If the principle of consultative communication is new to you, it could be a revelation. If you're an established dental professional, it will reinforce your belief in what you do and give you a different perspective on how to further improve your communication, performance and potential. Whatever area of dentistry you specialise in (or if you're a general dentist), one of the key areas where you need to be highly effective is communication and in particular understanding how to communicate in a consultative way. You and your team will also need to be able to gain the confidence of your patients and be able to "consultatively sell" the right treatment options for the patient. At some point in life, you will need to sell yourself, your ideas, your treatments, your business, your team, your products or services, or your opinion. You continually have to influence and persuade people. That is true for all of us. This book will show you how you can do that in a way that is truly consultative and enables you to engage more deeply with the people around you. If you apply what you learn in this book it will be beneficial to you and to everyone in your life.

If you've bought this book because you want to become a more highly skilled communicator, I commend you and thank you. This is a valuable investment in yourself, and one that will have a significant impact on your future – but only if you read, understand and apply what you learn. If you follow the instructions and the system, answer the questions, try the exercises and apply what you're learning, it will help you to become a more successful dental professional. What you learn in this book will also strengthen your relationships with your family, partner, children, friends, colleagues and patients. It will help you understand the people around you. It will stimulate your thinking and allow you to achieve things you never thought possible. It will help you attract opportunities for growth, development and, ultimately, success.

I hope your interest is piqued and that you're excited. You should be! Whatever your current circumstances, whatever your ambitions, get ready for a step change in your abilities and the most incredible future you can imagine.

Before we start, let's do a reality check. A lot of dental professionals are resistant to the idea of selling anything. They consider salespeople to be slimy, smarmy, pushy, selfish, crass, arrogant, obnoxious and insincere. If you've dealt with a lot of salespeople, you may hold this view. And if you've been sold to by an untrained salesperson, your opinion is likely to be justified. The truth is, 55% of salespeople have never been formally trained to sell and so they're putting a lot of their customers and potential customers off.

Many dental professionals haven't been trained in communication skills, and specifically, in consultative communication skills. While it might seem difficult and time-consuming to learn to communicate (and sell) in a consultative way, doing so significantly benefits them, their teams and their patients. And it's good for business growth too!

How this book came into existence

In 2001 I was sitting in a café just outside Kings Cross Station in London, England. I was speaking with a marketing colleague from the company I was working at as a Dental Key Account Manager, a title used for a salesperson who manages the strategic and larger customers for a business. I was sharing an idea I had with her about how we could help our customers who wanted to make the transition from NHS to Private Dentistry. The idea was to provide sales training for dentists to help them sell themselves and their private dental treatments and services. I'd been in dental sales for 8 years and attended a lot of sales training programs and have enjoyed helping many of my dental customers with useful hints and tips in the past. I'd been sketching on a pad for months and fleshing out an idea I had for a sales model in the form of a mnemonic, using the word INSPIRe.

This wasn't a sales model for sales teams, but a sales model that could help dentists and their teams 'INSPIRe' their patients to choose private dentistry (each letter of the word INSPIRe was a stage in the process).

As I shared the model with my colleague she said "this is really good Justin, so practical and simple. But it's not really something we could use as a company. It doesn't fit with what we're trying to do, and we wouldn't want to offer that as a service to customers, it would be a distraction to our team and the business". She was absolutely right. The other consideration was whether there was a sufficient demand for such a service, or sales training for dental teams. It was a completely new concept and would take a lot of work convincing the dental marketplace that there was a position for it. I was busy with my work and my career with the company was looking promising too. So, I parked the idea, but before I did, I took the notes I'd made, wrote them up in a word document, and saved the 'INSPIRe Sales System' in a folder called "Project ideas". I didn't look at it again properly until November 2017 when I left the corporate world and started to consider what my career options were.

In November 2017 I was burnt out, literally! I had spent 18 years working in many different Sales, Business and Leadership roles across different marketplace divisions for 3M. I found myself in the position of General Manager of one of their largest divisions in the UK. I was no longer enjoying my role and hadn't been for the last two and a half years. I needed a change and only realised how bad it had become when I burnt out. I won't go into the details, but this experience forced me to make a change in my work and life.

I left the corporate world and retrained as an Executive Coach with the AOEC (Association of Executive Coaching). I'd always enjoyed selling, coaching and leadership and so retraining as a coach was a fairly natural transition for me to make. I embarked on a 6-month program and found I now had quality time to invest in myself and my development, something I realised I'd neglected for too long.

I started planning how I was going to work as a coach and returned to my "Project Ideas" folder. I found the 'INSPIRe Sales System document and felt compelled to flesh out the INSPIRe model as it had been a simple overview back in 2001. I started to write chapter headings that aligned with the model and step-by-step it became a full program utilising the previous 27 years' experience of selling, coaching and leadership. At the same time, I started writing the 'INSPIRe Sales Manual' as a manuscript. Creating a program at the same time as writing a manuscript seemed to work well, one seemed to inform and compliment the other. By March 2018 The INSPIRe Sales System Training Program for B2B sales teams was ready to go!

Roll the clock forward to March 2020 and I had delivered the INSPIRe Sales Training program to twelve different sales teams, five of them were sales teams operating in the dental industry. The feedback was excellent, as were the results those teams gained following the program. Even the most experienced salespeople were saying how impactful the system was on their work. The demand for the program and my coaching was growing rapidly. Then the global pandemic struck!

Everything changed and my business was put on pause for about 3 months during the Lockdown 1.0 in the UK. I took the time to revisit my business and the programs I was offering and realign them to be relevant in both a physical and virtual environment, sales, coaching and leadership in the hybrid world. I also revisited the INSPIRe manuscript and was introduced to a publisher who helped me to publish the content in a book. In November 2020, INSPIRE, INFLUENCE, SELL – Master the psychology, skills and systems of the world's best sales teams was published.

In the first week of launch it became an Amazon best seller in the UK. I was flabbergasted and delighted!

I was part of a few dental networking groups, and a number of readers were dentists and dental professionals, as well as salespeople working in the dental market. I thought back to the original purpose of the model and the thought kept reoccurring to me – a consultative sales model for dentists. I'd also been working with an amazing team at the MiSmile Network for a while (a UK network of dental practices who are part of an ongoing program that helps them grow their Invisalign cases), I'd enjoyed sharing some of the ideas with their members that were directly from the INSPIRe model and from the INSPIRE, INFLUENCE, SELL book. I was also introduced to the BACD (British Academy of Cosmetic Dentists) and presented a webinar on consultative communication that had been very well received.

The idea for a revised version of the INSPIRe model to share best practices principles of consultative communication and sales was ignited. In May 2021 I started to reformat the content from my B2B sales programs and create the

INSPIRE, CONSULT, and SELL content. The first manuscript was ready in October 2021, I sent it to key Dental Leaders in my network and as they say, the rest is history.

A note about High Performance Principles

I have learned throughout my career that for any of us to be successful we must focus on three vital areas of performance: psychology, skills and systems. Psychology is the foundation of success in any field and will determine whether or not we believe we are able to succeed. Without belief, we cannot convince ourselves that we are capable of success. We will continually revisit the principles of positive psychology throughout this book.

Consultative Communicating & Selling is a learned skill and can be taught to anyone who is willing to learn and change the way that they work. I cannot emphasise enough the need for change. The world is changing rapidly. Your patients and their needs are changing almost constantly. The only way you can continue to be relevant to your patients is by changing the way you work. You must continually improve yourself so that you can meet their future requirements. In this book, I'll share with you a tried, tested and trusted way to improve your ability to communicate, influence and consultatively sell. If you adopt this approach, you'll become the best dental professional you're able to be, and in turn, surpass your patients' needs, now and in the future.

Consultative Selling is Serving

Some people have a hard time shaking the negative connotation that comes with the term sales, or the thought of selling. But if you consider "consultative selling" to be serving, you can start to think differently about it. When you're consultatively selling, you're helping your patients get a better understanding of their own needs, and you're helping them see that you're the best person to help them meet those needs. This shift in thinking can be liberating if you have any reservations about what consultative selling should be. You should be establishing a foundation that is ethical, honest and about serving your patient at the highest level possible – this is what separates 'the best in the dental market' from 'the rest of the dental market'.

This book will introduce you to the INSPIRe Consultative Sales System, a simple, powerful and effective system that will imprint on your unconscious mind so that you won't have to concentrate on remembering it. This system will naturally become your preferred consultative sales methodology. Throughout the book, you'll see specific references to the INSPIRe Consultative Sales System as well as more general references to the consultative sales process. This is intentional. It acknowledges the importance of structure and processes when it comes to successful consultative selling, whether through the INSPIRe System or a similar consultative sales process.

We'll also address motivation, the importance of changing behaviours and habits, and how to sustain improvements over the long term. If you're interested in quick fixes or wins, or better patient conversions, you'll see a definite improvement as a result of working through this book, but I ask you to dig deeper. Join me on the voyage of discovery and make a commitment to mastering the art of communication over the long term. The content of this book was born out of a passion for learning about success, high performance and personal transformation.

As I've already mentioned the INSPIRe Consultative Sales System came about through my own search for the most effective consultative sales methodology. I spent years altering and tailoring the techniques and principles of other communication and sales models in the corporate world because I couldn't find one that was simple enough to use consistently (without multiple aids and prompts) but comprehensive enough to make a real impact. I've amalgamated my skills and experience across sales, strategic account management, leadership, business strategy, coaching and NLP (neuro-linguistic programming) to create this book and the accompanying training that I deliver to dental organisations.

I started my career in dentistry as a dental technician in 1989. I qualified as a dental technician from Lambeth College, London and realised that I wanted more from my career. At the age of 22 I entered the world of dental sales working for a dental retail company based in Scotland. I then worked for the largest dental company in the world at the time and went on to become one of their highest performing sales professionals. In 1999 I joined 3M and that started a career in leadership then business management and saw me move outside of the dental market and gain experience in many different business sectors including Medical, IT Services, Commercial Graphics, Traffic Safety Systems and more. My career in sales and business spans over twenty-five years and I've worked with some incredible people and learned so much about how to lead high performance organisations. I'm fortunate to have extensive and quite unique experiences.

One common success factor I recognised was the ability to communicate, in particular to communicate in a consultative way. Consultative communication is learning about the person you are speaking with, listening deeply, asking quality 'consultative questions' and truly understanding them. Once you understand someone else, your ability to meet their needs, find agreement and commitment becomes a natural part of the communication flow. When you learn to communicate in a consultative way you become influential, you don't have to sell, persuade or direct people you inspire them.

That's what we'll be learning as we work through the INSPIRe Consultative Sales model. If you're working hard in your dental career but not reaping the results you know you should be, then working harder isn't the answer. Changing your approach using a tried and tested method, combined with hard work, will put you on a trajectory to success. I advise you not just to read this book but to work through it.

There are many opportunities to reflect and take action in ways that will support your development and strengthen your ability to inspire, consult and sell alongside your patients and team.

Whatever level of experience you have in dentistry, I'm confident you'll gain immense value from this book. It lays out a memorable consultative sales process over several chapters and also includes mastery content for each stage of the system, which will give you deeper insight and communication expertise. The combination of foundational and specialist material ensures that no matter where you're starting from, you can become a highly skilled communicator. You might want to work through this book at the foundational level for each chapter and return to the Consultative Sales Mastery section once you get to grips with the overall system and have developed your skills. Each chapter starts with an experience story in which I share relevant, valuable and sometimes funny anecdotes. If you prefer to dive straight into the sales system, you can skip that content. This book is designed to be accessible and flexible, so that you get the most out of it.

As you work through each chapter, I suggest you make notes in a journal or notebook. This will help you learn and adopt the content.

Let's start our journey together and your extraordinary transformation.

PART ONE

PREPARATION

Chapter 1: Consultative Selling: The Fundamentals

Consultative Selling Maxim:

"True Influence happens when what you want, and I want are the same."

When I first became a sales representative, in 1994, I worked for a medium-sized company based in Dundee, Scotland. It was a company that sold dental products to dentists, and I had previously worked as a dental technician. I remember how nervous I was starting at a new, larger company (the dental laboratory had four staff, and this company employed about 500). I had no experience in sales and even though I'd been a dental technician working in a practice-based dental laboratory, I knew little about the way dental practices used and ordered products.

I spent just one week in training at the Dundee head office, where I was introduced to key people in the organisation and trained on the products the company manufactured. I also spent two days in the field with members of their senior sales team covering different parts of Scotland. At the end of that first week, I was given the keys to my company car, a selection of the Yellow Pages that corresponded with my sales territory, a box of record cards and a fax machine. I was allowed to leave early (at 4.30pm) on Friday afternoon so that I could make the seven-and-a-half-hour drive home from Dundee. I got home late but still feeling a buzz about the exciting journey I was starting. I spent the weekend thumbing through the dental practices in the Yellow Pages, making my record cards and planning my journey for the first week on my new sales territory (previously vacant and unmanaged).

It was a true voyage of discovery. I worked for that company for almost two years, built some strong customer relationships and was fairly successful – without ever being taught how to consultatively sell. It wasn't until I moved to the next company that I was enrolled in a formal sales training programme with the company's sales trainer. I remember that the programme was comprehensive but complex and remembering all the elements of the training was difficult. But once I'd grasped the fundamentals of the model and practised being more consultative in my approach to communicating and selling, my confidence with clients and, more importantly, my results improved dramatically. I took what I'd learned and applied it to my client meetings. The difference it made in my ability to connect more deeply, understand my clients and meet their needs (whilst winning more business as a result), when I got it right, was revolutionary.

Become patient-centred in your approach

- To consultatively sell (or serve) effectively, you must prioritise and focus on your patient – even if it takes you longer or creates more work in the short term. This is a fundamental principle of consultative sales. Committing to meeting the needs of your patient gives you a huge competitive advantage. There are also countless positive side-effects, here are a few:
- Your mindset will shift to one of the ultimate services towards your patients.
- You will unconsciously communicate a deeper level of commitment to your patients.
- Any pressure you feel to 'convert the treatment' will be reduced.
- You'll foster stronger, more meaningful relationships.
- You will inspire greater loyalty from your patients.
- Your team will become more committed to delivering more value for your patients.
- You'll create authentic, genuine propositions that truly meet your patients' needs.

There is no downside!

If you start from this position and remind yourself (and your teams) that the most important perspective is always that of the patient, the experience you create will mean so much more for your patients (and your teams).

At every stage of interaction with your patients, ask yourself, 'If I look at this ONLY from my patient's perspective, how does it need to be?'

This reframing of your point of view will put you among the most caring and highest performing dental professionals on the planet!

The world changed forever in 2020 with the advent of the Covid-19 global pandemic. Whilst it proved difficult to navigate at first, there are many factors that have been immensely positive for the world of dentistry.

Five Vital Insights for Dental Professionals

The Zoom Effect

The Zoom Effect has meant business professionals spend a large portion of their working day looking at themselves on-line. This is unusual and many people haven't liked what they see. It's led to an explosion an explosion in demand for cosmetic dentistry.2

Demand for Cosmetic Dentistry & Aesthetic Treatments

The evidence shows that 1 in 10 adults in the UK has had cosmetic dental treatment in the last 12 months and the number seems to be rising. 3 Demand for 'patient led' cosmetic dentistry is going to be a driving force for growth in the dental marketplace.

2 The aesthetic Zoom Boom, Louis Malcmacher, Article for Dental Economics Sept 1st 2020
https://www.dentaleconomics.com/science-tech/cosmetic-dentistry-and-whitening/article/14183302/the-esthetic-zoom-boom
3 The Oral Health Foundation report 2020

UK household savings hit all-time high

An article by George Nixon for "This is Money" in 2020 cites a report by the ONS (Office for National Statistics) about the percentage of disposable income saved. The previous record of 14.4% was set in 1993 and was more than doubled in 2020 at a staggering 29.1%. The headline stated, "Britain becomes a nation of savers as Brits stash away 30% out of every £10 they could!"

It's safe to assume this is a contributing factor towards increased demand for cosmetic dental treatment.

Communication issues are a third of patient complaints

Communication problems are a common cause of complaints against dental practices. They account for around a third of complaints notified to the DDU. 4 In our changed modern world our ability to communicate effectively can be a great source of confidence and protection for ourselves, our patients, our teams and our business.

Communicate Effectively with patients

Communication in dentistry is such an important priority that it is directly stated in the GDC Focus on Standards. Principle No 2 is to communicate Effectively with patients. Give patients the information they need, in a way they can understand, so that they can make informed decisions. 5

3 The Oral Health Foundation report 2020

4 David Lauder – DDU Dentolegal Adviser, Dentistry Article 5th May 2020

5 GDC Standards for the Dental Team and Nine Principles for registered Dental Professionals

Communication is also a theme in many of the other nine principles.

My ten commandments of Consultative Sales

These commandments, combined with the right sales structure, show what it takes to be successful in consultative sales and in business. I teach them to many of my dental clients.

1. Focus entirely on your patient
2. Use a value-led approach
3. Tap into your intense passion
4. Continuously develop your expertise
5. Be exceptionally curious
6. Listen intently and create space
7. Enjoy the process and the results
8. Believe in your solution and yourself
9. Persevere until you succeed.
10. Gain commitment every time

I won't expand on these here, but throughout the book we'll look at them in the systems, stories and principles we cover.

Three important components of your patient proposition

As you have conversations with your patients, especially in early interactions before the relationship is fully established, your patients will be making an assessment about you and the services you offer.

To help you remember these simply, think about three P's: ***Person, Practice, Product***

Your patients will be assessing:

1 - You, the clinician:

- Can you be trusted?
- Will you deliver what they need?
- Are you knowledgeable, credible, engaged and likable?

2 - Your treatment options or service:

- Does your treatment or service deliver what they need?
- What is different or unique about it?
- Is it a brand they recognise or trust?

3 - Your organisation & team:

- Is your practice reputable?
- What is the feedback from other patients?
- What are the independent ratings of the treatments & services you provide?
- How well does the practice deal with issues, complaints or dissatisfied patients?

Your patient is looking to see if you, your treatment/ service and your organisation can be trusted to deliver what they need and if there is a 'fit' between you and them – they may not do this consciously, but they will do so intuitively. We'll cover how these fit within the consultative sales process, but at this stage, it's important to consider how you consistently represent yourself, your treatment options, and your organisation to give your patients confidence in these three priority areas. A gap in any one of these areas will create doubt for your patient and jeopardise your chances of gaining their confidence and ultimately being successful.

Your personal vision

As you work through this book, you'll learn many principles and practices that will help you hone your consultative communication skills. You'll set yourself personal goals. I also recommend that you create a personal vision of the dental/ business professional you wish to become. As an executive coach, I've worked with business leaders to clarify the visions they set for themselves and their organisations. While there are many different types of visions, two have stood out to me:

- Provide world-class service to my clients or patients
- Be the most trusted and respected provider to my clients or patients

Imagine if you made it your intention to be both 'world-class' and 'the most trusted and respected provider' to your patients. It will force a new level of thinking about how you operate. This is an incredibly high aspiration. I hope that when you consider this for yourself, you feel a mixture of emotions, as I do: a little fear, some scepticism, increasing curiosity and a swelling of excitement. Keep in mind that the achievements of every successful person, product and organisation were once no more than aspirations. This is where you are right now. If you identify your own personal vision and start living it from this day forward, you'll be setting a course for an astronomical breakthrough with your patients, your team and your practice or business.

I hope this discussion is already stimulating thoughts and ideas. Let's get started with the reflection. Take a moment now to write about your personal vision in your journal or notebook.

- What will inspire you to become the best dental professional possible?
- What do you want your patients to experience when they choose to have treatments with you?

You may also want to consider other points covered in this chapter and write about them. What are your thoughts and some possible actions you can take?

Chapter 2: The Power Of Change

Change Maxim:

"The ability to change is everything."

In recent roles leading business teams in organisations, I was approached to act as an adviser, or mentor, to people within the organisation who wanted advice on how to 'get on' in the company. While each person had different needs, skills, experiences and ambitions, similar themes emerged. In these discussions, the key point I emphasised was that without the openness, willingness and desire to change, you cannot develop, improve and achieve your future goals.

Remember, the ability to change is everything.

Once the person and I had established and agreed on the importance of change, the conversation would focus on three simple but powerful ideas:

- Commit to mastery and decide on a future role
- Gain future role experience immediately
- Set goals and take consistent action towards them

Let's look at each other more closely.

Commit to mastery and decide on a future role

First, you must commit to becoming the best you're capable of being in your current role. Becoming the go-to person – someone who is known to be an expert and who consistently delivers their best over the long term. There is no spotty performance, no slacking – always be delivering at the highest level and searching for ways to improve and stay at the top. Second, you must be clear on what you want your future role to be. For some, this might involve a promotion or even starting your own practice or business. In the right company, performing at your best gets you recognition, opportunities and even promotions or the offer of partnership. I appreciate there are exceptions to this, but it's worth remembering that even if this isn't true for your organisation, there is no downside to taking this approach. If you're focused on development, you'll become so valuable that you can move on elsewhere, if not within your own organisation. What's important is to define the future role. This will give you a point of focus – a target to aim for.

Gain future role experience immediately

I learned early in my career that it's difficult to be ready for your next role if you don't have experience doing it in some way. There is immense value in gaining experience in advance. It pushes you outside of your comfort zone, forces you to learn new skills, adds value to your business and prepares you for the future. There may be some pressure involved in the learning process, but this is fantastic preparation and life experience. It will make you a more well-rounded, confident person. Once you're clear on your next role, speak with your line manager and peers about your aspirations. They can help you find opportunities to step up and develop. Most people wait for a promotion opportunity and then get frustrated when they're overlooked, even though they haven't done anything tangible to prepare themselves.

Don't wait for the promotion to get the experience. Take action now. One other thing to consider – don't get hung up on being paid more or getting rewarded for taking on additional responsibilities. Money and rewards are guaranteed to come when you have the experience and are able to move upwards to that role. For now, appreciate the opportunity to develop yourself. Once you've learned a skill or gained experience, it is yours to keep no one can take it away. It becomes part of you, and that is priceless.

Set goals and take consistent action towards them

Once you're motivated to change, you're committed to being the best you can be, and you know what you want, set your goals and clarify the actions you'll take towards them. Setting and achieving goals is what separates high performers from the rest of the population. Make a habit of setting goals and taking action and it will pay you back tenfold over time. A number of goal-setting templates allow you to document and track your performance against your goals, including apps that you can use on your mobile, tablet or PC. Here's an example I use with my clients if you'd like a proven template:

https://bit.ly/Goal-Tracker-Dental

Goal-setting fundamentals

When setting goals, it's important to use positive statements, i.e., be clear about what you want rather than what you don't want. While this advice may sound obvious, it cannot be overemphasised. Our minds cannot process negative goals. The unconscious mind will work to achieve whatever you put your focus and attention on. While you can use consequences to spur yourself into action, you must not let them be the defined goal. Clearly state your goals (and write them down whenever possible) so that you give your mind (and your actions) a target. Consider these statements:

- I really don't want to miss my practice targets this year.
- I'm going to over-deliver by 10% against my practice target this year.

The second statement is much more effective. Even if you don't achieve the 10% growth over your target figure, your mind, your plan and your actions are firmly centred on overachievement. Repeatedly asking yourself how you will achieve the 10% over target will stimulate thoughts and actions that will drive you to greater success. Be conscious of the goals you set for yourself, and make sure you use positive statements when writing them down. This simple principle will revolutionise your results.

Your career journey

In my working life so far, I've had twelve different careers (including being an author/speaker/executive coach). While this number might sound high, it falls within an average. According to the Bureau of Labor Statistics, the average US worker will have 12.3 jobs in their working lifetime, and that number is rising. Workers now stay, on average, just four years in a role or an organisation.[3]

While companies are trying to figure out how they can keep employees loyal, employees are focusing on increasing their value so they're ready for change when the time is right.

The best way to prepare yourself is to acquire skills and experience that are aligned with the right area of speciality for you. Consider these four aspects, something; you enjoy, you're good at, that makes a positive impact for patients and is profitable for your practice. In Japan there is a principle called Ikigai. Ikigai is a framework that brings all four of these elements together.

3 'Number of jobs, labor market experience, and earnings growth: Results from a national longitudinal survey' [news release] (US Department of Labor Bureau of Labor Statistics, 2019), www.bls.gov/news.release/pdf/nlsoy.pdf, accessed 28 September 202026

Finding a way to embrace the Ikigai principles is said to create greater happiness, health, wellbeing, longevity and a deeper meaning.

If this interests you, look up the Ikigai model and consider how you can incorporate it into your practice and your development.

Remember, once you set your mind to it, you can achieve virtually anything: you just need the time, practice and determination to improve yourself every single day. With this commitment, you can become one of the highest-performing people in your field. Furthermore, you have a highly valued and transferable skill set.

My career has been a journey with numerous stops and changes along the way. Each part of the journey has formed the foundation for the next and given me a helping hand. As you develop skills and competence in one area, you'll naturally aspire to improve or challenge yourself further. This level of internal desire presents amazing opportunities for personal growth and satisfaction.

Initiating change

Changing our behaviours and habits can take a tremendous amount of effort, but the results are well worth it. Before we can change, we must be aware of and break through our existing blocks, resistance and forgetfulness. The well-documented "Ebbinghaus Forgetting Curve" describes how we lose memory of learned knowledge over time, with as little as 25% of knowledge retained after just six days. But with action planning, reflection, repetition, and coaching, this can be increased to as high as 90%.[4]

Through my client work and career to date, I've learned that to make lasting change, you must envision a powerful and compelling future and then clearly identify your personal motives (your motivation for change), capture them and revisit them regularly. Awareness of your resistance to change and a compelling reason to change will be a source of energy that keeps your motivation levels high. Throughout this book, you'll find opportunities to identify your reasons for change and actions you can take. This will help you gain clarity on your motivation and the ways in which you'll make that change happen.

Taking notes, reflecting on them and then committing to action will fuel your desire to improve and ensure your future success.

I recommend making a commitment to yourself in advance – a commitment that evokes a powerful emotional response in you. We'll revisit it often, so you're held accountable for changes and can access the best version of yourself.

4 H Ebbinghaus, Memory: A Contribution to Experimental Psychology (1885), available from CD Green, 'Classics in the history of psychology' (York University, no date), http://psychclassics.yorku.ca/ Ebbinghaus/index.htm, accessed 28 September 202028

Before we move on, reflect on this chapter and write down your thoughts in your journal or notebook.

- What level of performance would you like to reach?
- Why is it important that you embrace change and strengthen your skills?
- How will you keep yourself on track when you're busy or you lose focus?

Chapter 3: Setting Yourself Up To Win

Mindset Maxim:

"You must believe you can succeed before you can convince anyone else!"

Imagining a future that holds incredible success can be difficult and a little scary. Depending on your upbringing, self-image and unconscious programming, it can be stressful to think about a big change, even when that change is positive.

I've faced this challenge several times in my life. Whenever I'm looking to make a significant change, I'm aware that, on an unconscious level, it's going to require a considerable amount of effort. I'm not telling you this to put you off, but to get you in the right frame of mind – you need to get momentum and maintain it to make a lasting change. During these times in my life, I've worked through exercises like the one we'll look at now to help me create a clear vision of the future I want to achieve and to experience it in advance.

This is the best way to connect with and believe in the goal you've created. The exercise below will help you start to make an unconscious shift in mindset.

Visualisation

Done correctly and regularly, visualisation (i.e., mental rehearsal) can be a powerful tool to boost your confidence and, in turn, your success. We all visualise a lot of the time but don't always realise it. We also don't always realise how visualisation affects us and that we have the power to control our thoughts. With visualisation, you create the future in advance. And with routine practice and clearly defined outcomes, you can make visualisation an extraordinarily effective force in your life. Try it for yourself and see.

EXERCISE: WHAT DOES THE FUTURE LOOK LIKE?

Take a few minutes to write down in your journal or notebook why it's important for you to improve your performance in the future.

- To prepare for this exercise, I recommend doing this:
- Take five deep breaths – in and out.
- Think about a time in the future – at least a year from now. Imagine how you have transformed yourself: You are the highest-performing dental professional in your organisation.
- You have made an incredible impact on yourself and the people around you – your patients, family and friends.
- You have become recognised as highly accomplished and successful.
- You have unlocked the highest level of skill and experience.
- You have a strong sense of satisfaction, pride and achievement.

- Make notes in your journal or notebook.
- What does this look like?
- How does this sound?

- What are you feeling about yourself?

Now that you've experienced what it's like to go through this transformation, let's look at what you will have achieved. This is an opportunity to address key goal-setting areas and gain greater clarity about what success looks like to you.

Consider these areas to set yourself performance goals (you don't need to set goals in all these areas, but make sure you've set some in the areas most important to you):

- Finances (earnings, savings, investments)
- Family (your influence and example)
- Career/ business (roles available to you)
- Personal growth and development (skills you have mastered and are working on)
- Freedom (sense of flow and achievement)
- Time (working patterns and personal time)
- Life fulfilment (how you feel about yourself and your life)
- Mastery (being the best you can be)
- Your choice – what else is important to you?

Once you've captured these future performance goals, take a few moments to read through them and really connect with them.

Write down what you notice in your journal or notebook. These goals are going to be important for your motivation to change as we go through this book. They'll keep your engine running, especially when old habits and behaviour patterns try to resurface.

I recommend revisiting this exercise regularly to remind yourself of the change you want to produce in your life. This will keep you focused and motivated. You might want to take note of this page so you can come back to it.

Before we move on, reflect on this chapter and write down your thoughts in your journal or notebook.

Chapter 4: The High Performing Practice Model Prepare^2

Prepare Maxim:
"Preparation inspires Confidence & Performance!"

Having worked as a business manager, I know first-hand the importance of comprehensive preparation. Preparing our businesses is something different altogether, especially if we've been working in them for a long time. It can be overwhelming, complicated and time-consuming.

In 2017 when I set up my first business Focus4growth Ltd, I felt quite overwhelmed. There were so many things I needed to do to get the business up and running, in addition to passing my coaching diploma and gaining my coaching accreditation. After spending a lot of time writing lists, reading through my old corporate business plans and researching 'simple business plans' online, I went back to first principles. I asked myself "What are the priority actions I should take (and plan) that will make the biggest impact for me, my clients and my business?" I reflected on that question with each activity I started or planned to start, and it served me well. Of course, I still made plenty of mistakes along the way and was tempted by many distractions but returning to that question helped me refocus my efforts on the priority actions.

In the second year of my business, I started working with freelance assistants to help me with content writing, administrative tasks and social media management. Returning to this question and asking it of my "virtual team" seemed to help them gain clarity too. I've developed a simple framework that really seems to help prioritise my planning and actions and to track and monitor the progress of my business. It's an effective way to keep myself on track and communicate my priorities to my team, I've redesigned it for the business of dentistry and shared it with a number of clients. The feedback on it as a focus tool and a way to communicate priorities with the team has been excellent. I will share it with you alongside the questions I ask my clients to help them complete it for their own businesses/ practices.

The importance of preparation

I know that talk of preparation and planning can seem unnecessary, perhaps even boring. But conditioning yourself to allocate time for preparing and communicating your plans will help you and your team to perform at your best consistently and put you among the top 10% of the dental profession. A common misperception is that good businesspeople don't need to prepare – they just need to work hard or 'hustle'. While they may well achieve short-term results, doing this, they could double or even triple their performance if they invested time in preparation. Give yourself the opportunity to be in the top tier of dental professionals and businesspeople.

When you're occupied with a task, you adopt a state of mind without conscious effort or thought. This mental state may or may not be the 'ideal' state of mind with which to engage your patients. You can make a hugely positive impact on your performance simply by getting yourself into an enabling state of mind: one where you have an outlook and attitude that enables you to perform at the highest possible level. Your mindset is a vital component of success.

Revisit your performance goals. Now recognise that you'll achieve them faster if you develop the habit of preparing for each patient appointment or team interaction. In your journal or notebook, write 'The reason I need to prepare for each of my patient appointments (and team meetings) is…'

Then write down your reason.

Now that we understand why preparation is important, let's look at the High Performing Practice Model - The Prepare2 framework.

The framework

For many people, preparing for practice success can feel overwhelming. They don't know where to start, so they simply don't start. They don't do any preparation and risk feeling ill-prepared and then having to be reactive to events as they happen, which in turn drastically reduces their performance and success. If you or the team you manage aren't reaching the performance levels, you'd like and are having lower than anticipated patient treatment acceptance rates – i.e., the patient isn't choosing the treatment options you or your team recommend – it's likely to be one of two things. The first is poor preparation or the second is poor consultative communication or selling (remember selling is meeting you patient's highest needs).

Some business teams I've led in the past often didn't prepare because they made preparation more complicated and time-consuming than it needed to be. With the right framework, planning can be simple and powerful.

Over the years (and through many mistakes and successes), I identified four areas to focus attention on when preparing a business to deliver the optimal client experience or patient experience. I call it the Prepare2 (or 'prepare squared') framework and it really helps business & practice teams to increase performance, growth and results. See the diagrams below. Diagram 1 the overview of the framework. Diagram 2 is the detailed framework.

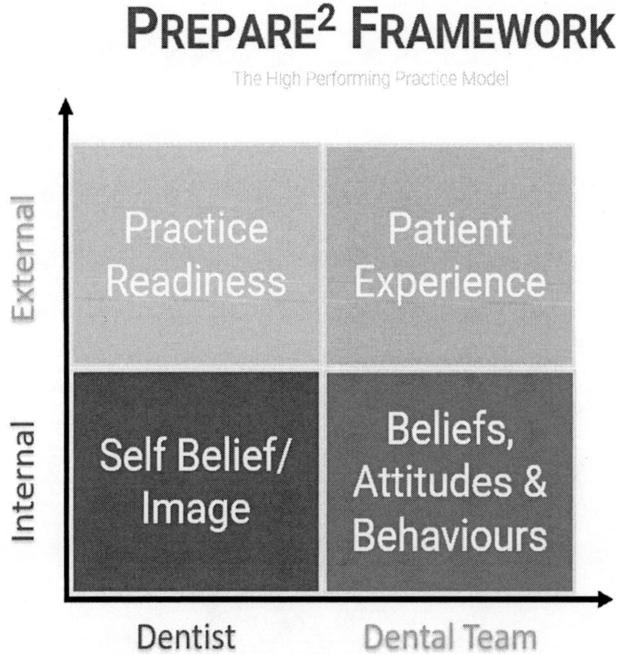

Prepare² Framework Overview:

The High Performing Practice Model

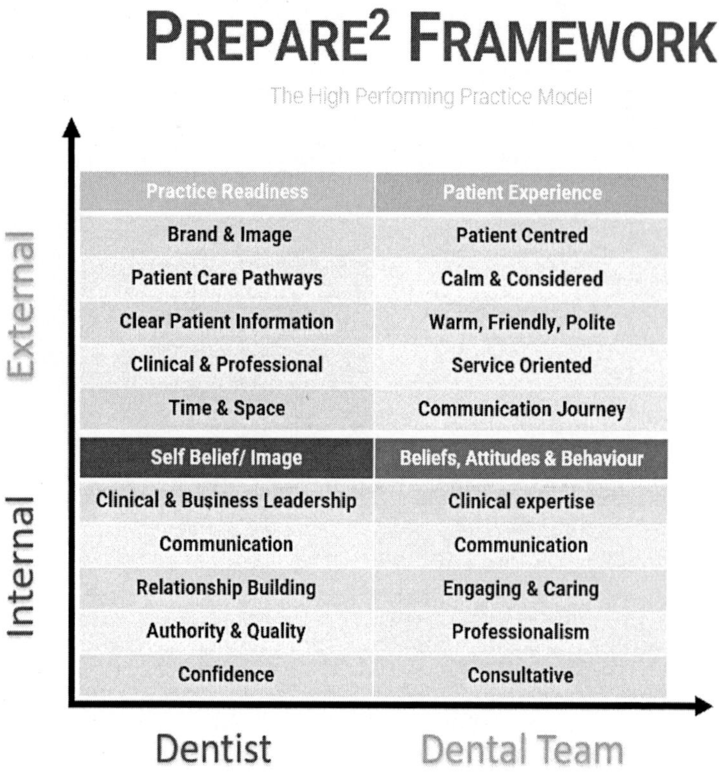

Prepare² Framework Detail:

The High Performing Practice Model

Before we go into the model, I've developed a tool I use with clients and on our INSPIRE, CONSULT, and SELL programs. The tool is a simple action planner that you can work with to identify your key actions, document them and track your progress. I'm providing a copy of it for you to download and use here: https://bit.ly/High-Performing-Practice. With your blank plan ready, let's look at each of the areas of the High Performing Practice Model.

Dentist/ Dental Professional

As Dental Professionals we spend a lot of time on professional development. Improving our clinical skills, learning new techniques and procedures, understanding best practice and new product innovations amidst the running of a busy dental surgery and practice. For Dental Professionals, the treatment of patients and the leadership of our assistants and teams is a critical area to prioritise. Without personal development it's easy to feel anxious or undermined at times and that can lead to a crisis of confidence.

When we work in our own practices and businesses, we can become blinkered to the reality of our surroundings and the way we present ourselves to and the outside world. We inadvertently find ourselves working hard and repeating the same tasks and routines day to day, week to week, month to month and so on. Before we realise standards are starting to slip, we become oblivious to the opportunities for us to improve the environment and things plateau.

We address both of these priorities on the left-hand side of our framework, let's look at each quadrant in turn.

Internal – Self Belief

Starting with ourselves and building self-belief is an important factor in our ability to perform, especially if we aim to operate at our best and provide leadership for our practice team. Even if you're not the principal of the practice, building your self-esteem, self-belief, confidence should be an ongoing part of your personal development. For many people self-belief is not something they've worked on, and it leads to under-performance without them even realising it. There are simple, practical actions we can take on a regular basis that help us build self-esteem and confidence. It doesn't happen by accident; it has to be by intention. You, or someone you may know might struggle with confidence, the root cause is self-belief.

Here are some useful questions and exercises that will help you develop self-belief and identify personal development priorities.

Clinical & Business Leadership
When you think of your position as both clinical and business leader, whatever your formal title.

- How confident are you in your business leadership abilities?
- How confident are you in your clinical practice?

- How are you aligning with your team?
- What are your key development areas, (clinical & business leadership)?

Communication

When you consider communication, consider clarity and frequency to ensure your patients and team understand the message received and is aligned with the message delivered.

- How often do you communicate with the practice team?
- What key messages do you present?
- How often do you review 1:1 with your direct reports?
- How often does each member of the team review?

Relationship Building

Relationships are vital in practice; we will go the extra mile for someone we like and trust. That trust must be earned by us as leaders.

- How well do you know each member of the team?
- How would you rate your relationship with your team?
- What do you do to regularly invest in relationships?
- When did you last praise each member of your practice team?

Authority & Quality

At times it's important that we direct and steer our teams in order to raise standards and help them embrace the improvement opportunities that they can't see for themselves.

- How would your team describe your leadership authority?
- On a scale of 1-10 how would your team rate the quality of your leadership?
- How would your patients describe your authority as a practitioner?
- On a scale of 1-10 how would your patients rate the quality of treatment?

Confidence

Priming ourselves and accessing resourceful emotional states only happens when we focus our attention and energy. Consider your normal work week.

- How confident do you feel in clinical practice?
- How confident do you feel when you're leading your business?
- How confident are you in challenging your team when needed?
- How confident are you in challenging your peers when needed?
- What are you doing to build your self-confidence?

Action Steps:

Identify your key actions to improve your Self Belief Discuss with your team as it will help them too.

- Agree with your Key Changes
- Capture one action per category on the worksheet.

Note; If you want to go deeper into this area, we have a free client programme called 'Cultivate your Growth Mindset'. Here is the link to enrol, it's free and more than 300 people have worked through the content. The feedback is excellent and the improvement in self-confidence for many participants has been transformational: https://bit.ly/Mindset-Programme

External – Practice Readiness

This stage is about becoming more intentional about the external presence and projection of your organisation, yourself and your team to the outside world. It's important to take a step back, detach ourselves and look at our practice, team and services with an objective viewpoint. This is the only way we can identify the opportunities for improvement.

Let's review some key questions that will help identify the key areas to focus on.

Brand & Image

Take an objective view of the practice, consider the 'experience' of:

- Reception / Non-Clinical Areas
- Patient Waiting Areas
- Surgeries/ Clinics/ Exam Rooms
- Team - appearance & attitude
- Conversations – direct and indirect

Patient Care Pathways

If you consider the view of the practice, team and services through the 'eyes of your patients'.

- How intentionally have you designed your 'patient journey'?
- How well has it been communicated with your team?
- How much does your team believe in it?
- How well do they (& you) represent it?
- How does it feel to be a patient?
- What should it feel like?

Clear Patient Information

When patients are learning about treatments and their care pathway for the first time, consider Key Treatment Options…

- What Patient information do you have for them?
- Do all of the team understand the options available?
- Are they able to discuss them?
- Are they supportive of them?

Clinical & Professional

With Dental Professionals working in practice, considering you and your team.

- Are CPD records up to date?
- What are the key areas of non-clinical professional development?
- How good is communication with patients and other team-members?
- Who gives direction and guidance?

Time & Space

For Private Practice, or aspiring Private Practice, consider these questions.

- As a patient can I tell the difference between an NHS and private experience?
- How much more time is allocated for private patients?
- What are the patients' expectations?
- How well are they being met by the team?
- As a patient, do I feel my investment is worthwhile?

Action Steps:

Identify your key actions to improve Practice Readiness. Discuss with your team as it will help them too.

- Agree with your Key Changes
- Capture one Action per category on the worksheet.

The Dental Team

On the right-hand side of our model, we consider the team that works alongside us in practice. It doesn't matter how well we perform as an individual, if the team around us isn't well aligned, taking a similar approach and committed to working the way we've agree to work, then the practice will not meet its full potential.

On this side of the framework, we review our team's internal beliefs, attitudes and behaviour as well as the experience that it creates for the patient. As practice leaders, we must take ownership of the way our team performs, and that empowers us to inspire change. If we dismiss team performance or see it as out of our control, then we are accepting poor performance and that inevitably impacts the patient experience and over time the business results.

Again, let's work through the quadrants one at a time.

Internal - Beliefs, Attitudes & Behaviours

In this quadrant we are focusing on the standards of our team in practice. When you consider the patient experience and interactions with our team, the poorest performer becomes the weakest link in the chain. As leaders in the practice and peers of other professionals, we have an opportunity (and obligation if we're owners and partners) to ensure team is performing at the highest level possible and fulfilling their highest potential.

As with the previous quadrants let's review some key questions that will help identify the key areas to focus on.

Clinical Expertise

- What is the level of clinical expertise of each of the teams?
- What gaps exist?
- What are the clinical fundamentals that every member of the team should have?
- What training or coaching should be provided to fill the gaps?

Communication

- How well does each member of your team communicate with patients?
- How well do they communicate with each other?
- What training has the team had on effective communication?
- How often is the teams' communication reviewed and improved?

Engaging & Caring

- How engaged is your team in their work and serving patients?
- How well does your team provide genuine patient care?
- How empathetic is your team towards patients who are apprehensive?
- How well do you and your team 'read' patients emotional states?

Professionalism

- On a scale of 1-10 how would you rank your team's professionalism?
- What are the principles, standards and values for your practice?
- When did you last communicate them to your team?
- What review process is in place to maintain standards?

Consultative Approach

- On a scale of 1-10 how would you rank the professionalism of your team?
- What are the principles, standards and values for your practice?
- When did you last communicate them to your team?
- What review process is in place to maintain standards?

Action Steps:

Identify your key actions to improve the beliefs, attitudes and behaviours of the practice team.

- Discuss with your team to get their input too.
- Agree with your Key Changes
- Capture one Action per category on the worksheet.

External – Patient Experience

There is an argument to say that nothing else matters as much as the patient experience. Without an intentional, consistent and outstanding patient experience then your practice will never be excellent, and it will not fulfil its true potential. When we invest our time in creating and continually improving the patient experience, we become highly attractive to patients. Our teams have become more invested in their work and proud to represent the practice and our services. This only happens when we become intentional about our patient's experience.

For this final and arguably most important quadrant, let's review some key questions that will help identify the key areas to focus on.

Patient Centred - As a Patient visiting the practice

- How 'special' do I feel through every contact with the practice team?
- What are the things I notice that make me feel important?
- What are the magic moments that reassure me?

Calm & Considered - Considering the patient's perspective

- What measures are in place to create a calm atmosphere?
- How well do the team 'intentionally' project calm to patients?
- What should patients notice that would help them feel relaxed and confident?

Warm, friendly & polite - In practice team interactions

- How consistent is the approach of every team member?
- Are all team members appreciative of patients?
- What guiding principles for patient communication are in place?
- How often are they revisited?

Service Oriented - The team's approach to service

- How pro-actively does the team try to deliver first class service?

- How often is the team making suggestions to improve service?
- What measures are in place to ensure patients can provide feedback on their experience?
- What is the improvement cycle in practice?

Communication Journey - As a patient attending the practice

- How is the communication?
- Before, During & After treatment
- How easily do I understand the treatment options & the pathway?
- How consistent is the experience?
- What are the obvious gaps?

Action Steps:

- Identify your key actions to improve the Patient Experience.
- Discuss with your team and gain their input and commitment.
- Agree your Key Changes
- Capture one Action per category on the worksheet.

If you've completed this exercise and used the worksheet, you should now have some insightful and valuable ideas and action steps. Remember, business success is a team sport! These actions should be distributed to the most appropriate members of your team, not just you! Avoid assigning actions to 'all'. Without ownership of the action, it will not be completed and followed up. Pin a badge of accountability on a member of the team for every action that is in the plan. Remember to have a conversation with them about the action and why it's important that it's completed, then follow up.

Consultative Sales Mastery: Preparing yourself for success

Personal preparation

To be at your best, you must tap into your most resourceful state of mind. Before an important competition, athletes get themselves into a zone or a state of flow to heighten their performance. You can do the same.

Here's a proven way to create this powerful, positive state of mind. I recommend doing this preparation immediately before every interaction you have with a patient. Complete this exercise as a starting point, and then revisit it before each patient appointment to create a positive experience for you and your client.

- In your journal or notebook, write the answers to these questions:
- Who does your patient need you to be in order to choose you?
- What attitude and mindset do you need to adopt to be at your best?

- Think of a time when you were at your best – confident and in the zone. What did you see, hear, feel or say to yourself?
- Imagine the perfect interaction with your patient. Both of you are enjoying the discussion, and the patient thanks you for supporting them to make the right decision. Capture what you see, hear, feel and say.

Take a few moments to read through your responses. Allow the full potential of this exercise to resonate with you. Become aware of how excited and positive doing so makes you feel.

Capture what you notice in your journal or notebook.

The importance of this preparation ritual will become apparent once you start using it as part of your personal practice. You'll be able to consistently bring your best self to your patients and your team. And they will notice this and appreciate your intention to be your best self for their benefit. While it takes effort at first, if you prepare this way for every patient interaction for the next three weeks, you'll not only realise the benefits but also create a habit that will take over. You'll no longer have to think about doing this. In fact, it will seem easier to prepare than to 'wing it'.

Simply returning to this page and reading your notes will help you to develop this ritual and form a positive habit for the future.

EXERCISE: TAKE TIME TO VISUALISE

Below is another simple visualisation script. Read through it to familiarise yourself with it, and then follow the instructions.

Relax and take three deep breaths. When you're ready, close your eyes and imagine this:

1. You're at the end of the appointment with your patient.
2. You're both smiling as you say goodbye.
3. The appointment/ treatment has gone better than you expected.
4. The patient shared a number of relevant priorities and challenges with you.
5. You understand exactly what your patient needs.
6. Your patient agreed you were the one who could help.
7. You have agreed to a treatment plan that will deliver their ideal outcome and you know you'll enjoy providing the treatment and seeing the results.
8. Notice how good this feels and what you see, hear, experience and say to yourself.

I hope you enjoyed this activity. Remember, when you practise visualisation regularly, it will become a formidable force in your preparation for patient appointments and treatment.

You're now ready to work through the INSPIRe Consultative Sales System. But before we move on, reflect on this chapter and write down your thoughts in your journal or notebook.

PART TWO

LAYING THE FOUNDATION

Chapter 5: The INSPIRe Consultative Sales System

Process Maxim:

"We can't reproduce success without a process to follow!"

During my many years working in the dental marketplace as a salesperson, key account manager and sales manager, I received training on countless different sales programs. Some of the content was excellent, and I gained useful insights that helped shape my performance and career. Having been resistant to the thought of selling early in my career, I was learning that true consultative sales was different. It was about understanding what my client really needed and knowing in detail what service I was able to provide. While there was a strong positive match between the two, it was my ability to communicate in a way that the client found compelling that made the sales process work.

I realised that early in my career (when I wasn't very good at selling) I'd been inadvertently trying to push, persuade and convince my customers to buy from me. As I learned how to consultatively sell, I realised that it should be about being curious, learning, listening and then inspiring my clients to work with me, not just buy from me.

All change must come from the inside out! We can't persuade someone to do something they don't want to do or buy something they don't want to buy. And we shouldn't try either! Rather, we should understand what they really need, and then see if we can meet those needs. It won't always be the case, and if we're honest about that, our credibility and reputation will improve rapidly.

I remember having numerous conversations with dentists who were clients and became friends about the principles of selling to patients. I was complimented many times by my clients, they would say things like "Well, you're not really selling to me though are you, Justin?"

They were absolutely right about the relationship, they were genuine and as you'll learn from our model, building relationships is a central component of the consultative selling process. Another principle that's important is that as the client (or patient) it should never feel as though you are being sold to. If you ever feel as though you're pitching or that you're trying to sell a treatment, you're taking a wrong approach.

I remember being asked to share some consultative selling principles with a dental client of mine and her team (early in my development of the INSPIRe process). I explained the steps we'll be learning and shared some principles to apply when having conversations with her patients. At the start of each chapter in the process, I'll be sharing those principles alongside a relevant story.

The result for this client of mine was that she and her team were more confident and capable in their conversations about treatments with patients. Their private case acceptance rates increased dramatically, and all they did was change the way they discussed treatment options. By sharing a process with them they could then follow the steps, and that allowed them to be consistent in their approach and effectively deliver the result that both the patient and the dentist desired.

The use of a simple mnemonic model is not new, and in the world of coaching there is a simple, yet powerful model that has become the gold standard. This model is used the world over and is recognised as the framework that underpins many coaches' work with clients. I started to use the model with my team, family and friends and found it remarkable. It works every time. It's called the GROW model.

Here's a summary of the GROW model:

G – Goal (What is the client's goal?)

R – Reality (What is the client's current reality?)

O – Options (What options does the client have?)

W – Will (What will the client commit to do now?)

This model is so well used that it has been expanded and adapted by various coaching organisations. A recent enhancement is To GROWME, which broadens the scope of the coaching discussion:

To – Topic (What is the priority topic of the coaching session?)

G – Goal (What is the client's goal?)

R – Reality (What is the client's current reality?)

O – Options (What options does the client have?)

W – Will (What will the client commit to do now?)

M – Monitor (What will the client do to stay on track?)

E – Evaluate (How will the client know that they've been successful?)

I have successfully used the GROW and To GROWME coaching models (as have thousands of other coaches and leaders) because they are simple and effective. When I started using these models, I wondered, 'Why isn't there a similar simple and effective model for consultative selling?' I searched through my previous sales training manuals, had discussions with colleagues and explored the internet but couldn't find a model that I believed would truly deliver what business teams and leaders needed, regardless of market or role.

So, I developed my own. It's simple enough to recall instinctively yet comprehensive enough to be of use to all sales professionals, regardless of their experience.

The INSPIRe Consultative Sales System is the result of over twenty years of experience in sales, sales leadership, business management, coaching and training inside and outside of dentistry and medical markets. Over the last 3 years it has become trusted by many business teams and business leaders. Since 2020 it's returned to its original purpose, to help dental professionals have consultative discussions with patients so they make the most informed treatment selection. The INSPIRe model is more than a communication and consultative selling, it will help you strengthen the important relationships in your life.

In all the years I served as a sales and business leader, I never found a system that delivered what the INSPIRe Consultative Sales System does: the psychology, the skills and the process. Since its inception, the INSPIRe System has been known only to a select few high-performing sales & business teams who work with me and the Focus4growth team. When selecting clients for training and coaching on the system, we ring-fence customers in key segments, so that they get access to a true competitive advantage. The system has become a valued secret among those key clients.

With the publication of this book, I am sharing the secret to help countless teams and leaders dramatically improve their consultative communication and business performance. This is a fundamental part of my mission: to transform leadership, inspire teams and create legacies in organisations and communities around the world. I'm delighted to let you in on the secret.

When we inspire someone, we infuse into their mind. We connect and communicate with them deeply, enabling us to influence and engage them in a way that is incredibly valuable. As you review the INSPIRe Consultative Sales System, I encourage you to keep this representation of the system ever present in your mind. To be an inspirer to your patients and your team.

The acronym INSPIRe is a mnemonic. Here it is in full:

INSPIRe – Consultative Sales System
(Rapport and Relationship)

I – Insight and Impact

N – Needs Discovery

S – Solution Discussion

P – Proposal Agreement

I – Initiate Action

Re – Reflection

The acronym will help you remember, on an unconscious level, the 'right' process when it comes to consultative communicating and selling. It's critical to get the process right – you must perform the right tasks in the right order. I like to use the analogy of flat-pack furniture. You can wing it, but if you don't follow the step-by-step instructions, you inevitably end up with something in the wrong place or the wrong way around or with pieces left over. Consultative Selling is exactly like that. If you don't follow a process, you're likely to miss something important that your patient needs to make a decision.

Get comfortable with the process

Many dental professionals who don't follow a process for communicating justify this decision by saying they're worried they will come across as sounding scripted. Don't be concerned, actually using a structure makes us seem more confident and in control. It's true that when you first start following the process, you may have to concentrate on it – but that's why we use a mnemonic. The acronym makes it easy to remember the order and flow. Once you've practised it (and I recommend that you do, through the exercises in each chapter) and it becomes engrained, you won't have to consciously think about it. You will flow through your process. And once you have it committed to your unconscious memory, you will naturally better understand and meet your patients' needs. And you will have more patients accepting treatment recommendations and you will gain more business.

For those of you who prefer a visual representation, the flow chart below shows how the process works.

INSPIRe – Consultative Sales System

As you can see from the diagram, the process is designed to be ongoing and continuous. It will help you establish a methodology that you can use in all your interactions with people, whether it's a patient appointment, team member review or as part of building a long-term relationship with a partner or peers. You may also have noticed that in the system's second, third and fourth stages, the process flows in both directions. INSPIRe is a fluid system, and each stage must be completed before the next can be successfully progressed through. If you get stuck or your patient is resisting, orient yourself to this system and return to the stage that's necessary to get you and your discussion back on track. You will find answers simply by letting the system guide you.

Once the process is imprinted in your mind, whether you use the acronym or the flow chart or a combination of the two, you will be able to relax and be yourself in your consultative conversations with your patients and teams.

Consultative Sales Mastery: Understanding different personality types

Whilst the consultative approach is an enabler of better conversations, we must also appreciate that we are all different. We think and behave differently, and we all interpret the world around us in a particular way. When we're approaching consultative conversations with patients and team members, taking the time to consider their personality type can be valuable. There are many different ways to assess personality and we won't look at the different models here. We will discuss four principles that will help you understand yourself and better recognise patient's and team-members preferences so you can communicate more effectively with them.

The Four areas we're going to focus on are:

Introvert vs Extravert and Big Picture vs Detail Oriented.

Introvert vs Extravert

Introverted people prefer quiet spaces, they like to take their time to make a decision and they generally want more information before they make a decision. They like to mull things over, and they don't want to be pressurised to decide any more quickly than when they're ready. Introverted people think and process their thoughts before they speak. The other key insight about introverted people is that when they spend time with other people it drains their energy, and time alone recharges their energy. A day mixing and talking to other people can be exhausting for an introverted person. They won't always feel confident to ask questions, especially if they feel under pressure. When dealing with introverted people – slow down, give them space to think and process their thoughts, they will appreciate it.

Extraverted people are the opposite of introverted people. They prefer things a little faster paced, they like the hustle and bustle of a busy environment, and they tend to be quicker to react and respond. Extroverted people tend to talk as they think, and at times it can appear to be a constant stream of consciousness. Being with people energises them. On the whole, extraverted people tend to ask more questions and tell you if they need more information. They are also quicker to make decisions once they have all the information they need. They prefer a conversation to be at a faster pace and want to get things agreed more quickly.

Big Picture vs Detail Oriented

Big Picture thinkers are people who focus on results and outcomes, they know what they want and they're keen to get it. They want a picture painting of the final outcome and will be much more convinced by patient case studies and testimonials from other patients. They will know a little about a lot of things and will scan the headlines, rather than know the details. When dealing with the Big Picture, people spending too long talking about the details can turn them off. Once they have the information they need, they want to get on with the next steps and make progress towards the outcome.

Detail Oriented people need to know the nuts and bolts before they'll make important decisions. They want to know the step-by-step process and what happens at every stage. They may ask about materials and details that may even seem irrelevant to most of us. Being guided through the steps carefully and having resources they can take away and read and research will help the detail-oriented person to be confident to make a decision. Given that just the Big Picture leaves them feeling as though there is a huge gap in their knowledge and confidence.

As we're dealing with patients and our teams, we will encounter people who are at the opposite ends of each of these spectrums and at all stages in between. We must learn to recognise the signals from the other person and adapt our approach. Not doing so risks a conflict in our understanding of the other person and a miscommunication. If in doubt, slow things down, ask them questions and you'll soon start to build a picture of how they perceive the world around them. Once you have an idea of their preferences you can have a more meaningful and impactful consultative conversation with patients and team-members alike.

You'll have been thinking about your team members, partners, patients and even friends and family members as you read this section.

Before we move on, reflect on this chapter and write down your thoughts in your journal or notebook.

Consider, what changes do you need to make to your approach with key people, or types of people?

Chapter 6: Overcoming Challenges

I was working as a sales and marketing manager in a healthcare company. At this point, I had many years of experience under my belt and was well regarded by the organisation and our clients. The organisation had several business development managers (BDMs) who manage large healthcare business accounts. One of the BDMs (we'll call her Grace) secured an important meeting with a procurement director acting on behalf of a customer group. Grace was taking the lead on a procurement project, and the objective of the customer group she was targeting was to identify the lowest-priced, 'fit for purpose' product in a specific category. We were the higher-quality market leader, the group's predominant supplier and among the most expensive. The procurement director (let's call her Roberta) was renowned for being demanding and challenging, and neither of us had met her before.

We prepared for the meeting thoroughly and developed numerous questions and a draft proposal that we believed would be compelling. We arrived at the meeting ahead of time and were well briefed, prepared for anything the client could throw at us.

The meeting did not go well!

Roberta did everything in her power to impede our attempts at creating rapport. She scowled all the way through the meeting and snarled when we introduced humour, kept her arms folded, shook her head on every occasion and kept her answers to all of Grace's high-quality questions (more on those later) short and sharp. It was one of the toughest client meetings I've ever experienced – uncomfortable, negative and disheartening.

Roberta's position in a nutshell was that in order for the group to make savings, they couldn't stay with the incumbent – they had to move to a low-priced supplier. I believe we made a compelling case and did everything possible in that meeting. We discussed the costs of change, we provided evidence of the support our sales and clinical teams provided to the group's accounts, and we had referrals from senior clinicians across the group who were determined to keep using our products because they firmly believed we were the best supplier. Roberta was unmoved. I'm convinced she'd made up her mind before the meeting – no matter what, we were out!

Our final discussion was about patient safety and included a review of the valuable work our teams had been doing alongside clinicians in their group to improve standards and consistency of care and reduce risk for patients. When I mentioned that these initiatives couldn't be supported by a low-priced competitor (which this competitor subsequently confirmed to Roberta), she said, 'That's a risk I'm prepared to take.' That was the point at which we agreed to wrap up the meeting and leave.

I later learned that this meeting was typical of Roberta's style. Over the next few years, the procurement project didn't gain much traction. The wider group didn't appear to support the decisions made and apparently saw Roberta as someone who made cynical, biased recommendations. My organisation's business didn't change much across the group, but the proposal we made to them would have delivered significant savings for their organisation.

I also learned that in one meeting, Roberta rejected a significant savings proposal in favour of a cheap supplier and terminated an existing agreement (and was rude to a senior manager). Within a couple of months, the product from the cheap supplier was failing. The supplier then ran out of stock. Roberta had no choice but to instruct her team to start sourcing from the original supplier at a much higher price. This is an awful example of how a limited number of procurement people operate. When they don't create working partnerships with their suppliers, they can increase their organisational costs.

Learning from difficult clients & patients

We all have difficult clients and/ or patients, and as the saying goes 'you can't please all of the people, all of the time', it's impossible. But looking back on this I'm grateful for the experience I had with Roberta and other difficult clients. These experiences have made me much more aware of how difficult some clients can be, and that I shouldn't take it personally. It is also a reminder that sometimes, you just need to accept a situation and move on to the next, more appreciative, client or patient.

So, before we start working with the INSPIRe Consultative Sales System, take this opportunity to think about difficult patient situations you've found yourself in. Identify what happened and prepare yourself to better handle these types of encounters in the future. Learning to trust the consultative sales system and the skills you develop will really help.

Think of a specific patient interaction that didn't go the way you wanted it to. Now keep these questions in mind and reflect on them as you continue to work through the book. You may want to write them down in your journal or notebook so they're handy.

- What was the challenge with the patient?
- Which part of the system might I have been missing?
- What should I focus more of my time on when it comes to my patients?
- What am I learning about how I currently communicate with patients compared to the model?
- What changes can I make?
- What impact would this have on my future performance?
- What am I committed to changing?

Consultative Sales Mastery: Your inner voice

Patient perspective

Often, we'll be preparing for appointments with new patients, or with patients we're looking to discuss complex treatment options. There's usually a lot going on in our minds. Our 'inner voice' gets loud and can default to a negative perspective. We might ask ourselves these types of questions:

- ➢ What if they don't trust me?
- ➢ How do I give them confidence in me?
- ➢ What if they ask for something I can't give them?
- ➢ What mood will they be in?
- ➢ What do I say if they challenge the price?

These thoughts can create stress and pressure and, in turn, impair your performance in the appointment. A simple way to overcome this is to put yourself in your patient's shoes. To gain a new perspective and feel more at ease going into your appointments, follow these simple steps:

- ➢ Imagine you are your patient, in the time before the appointment with you.

Ask yourself:

- What do I want to get from this appointment?
- How do I want to be treated by the dentist?
- What am I most afraid of?
- What would win me over?

- What is my ideal outcome?

Capture your answers in your journal or notebook and consider how these insights might improve your meeting.

This worksheet will be a useful template as we work through the INSPIRe Consultative Sales System:

https://bit.ly/INSPIRe-Worksheet-ICS

Managing your inner voice

Each of us has an inner voice, and it chatters away most of the time. It's your cheerleader when you're doing well, and it can be your most fearsome critic when you're not. It's not something people tend to talk about or confront often, but because it can be distracting, we must spend time improving it and learning to use it more effectively. In NLP research and theory, a number of principles explain how the mind works. One of them is that every behaviour has a positive intention. This is particularly true when it comes to your inner voice. However critical you may find the voice, the intention behind it is always positive. For example, when you put yourself in a difficult situation, your mind will always try to protect you. It will either help you prepare or try to get you to avoid the situation altogether. Unfortunately, the inner voice isn't always useful or empowering, even though that's the intent.

With awareness, time and practice, you can turn your inner critic into your inner coach – a voice that supports you and helps you improve. It can become one of your most powerful and positive allies in your career and your life.

When I'm feeling frustrated with myself, my inner voice will generate rapid-fire negative comments or questions, such as:

- This happens all the time. You're useless.
- How did you get into this mess?
- How much worse can this get?

As soon as I notice the pattern of questions, I catch myself. I stop the thoughts, take a deep breath, check my posture and ask an empowering question, such as:

- Thank you. There's something here for me to learn. What is it?
- What is the positive intention in this for me?
- How can I use this to make myself even better in the future?

By making the effort to increase your awareness, you can leverage your inner voice. It's well worth it. Below are four simple steps to help you handle your inner voice:

1. Notice what your inner voice is saying.
2. Acknowledge and thank your inner voice (this takes the power away and gives you control).
3. Ask yourself, 'What is the positive intention in this for me?'
4. Then ask, 'What is the best outcome I can get from this now?'

If this is particularly relevant to you, I urge you to research further.

I will also repeat the link for the Growth Mindset programme here, it addresses the management of the inner voice in detail. You can sign up here, it's completely free of charge:
https://bit.ly/Mindset-Programme

Before we move on, reflect on this chapter and write down your thoughts in your journal or notebook.

6 If you would like to learn more about NLP there are many resources available online. Simply search for 'NLP' and you will be surprised at just how much information, training and content is available.

Chapter 7: Building Rapport & strengthening relationships

Rapport & Relationship Maxim:
"We won't buy from people we don't like!"

INSPIRe – Consultative Sales System:
Rapport & Relationship

When I first learned about rapport and relationships as a fundamental part of selling and influencing, it was an important discovery for me. I realised that people like people who are like them. They also like people who are interested in them (read the last two sentences again). At the start of a relationship, it's critical to show interest. I remember using this principle with an important new key account customer I was responsible for managing. The first time I had met with him we hadn't 'connected' at all. He had issues with the service my predecessor had been providing and his trust in the company – and by virtue, me – was compromised. At the end of the first meeting the atmosphere was frosty.

At the next meeting I focused solely on building rapport and gaining his trust. As soon as I arrived at his office, and we were introduced again I made a conscious effort to act and behave in a similar way to him. I asked questions about him, his work and his team. I asked questions that uncovered the challenges in the previous relationship and questions that led him to tell me how I could 'reset' our relationship. I kept the questions focused on a positive affiliation for both parties, while actively being interested and 'like him'. All the time, I matched his pace, tone, body language and gestures. During the course of the meeting our connection strengthened.

The result was astounding. Over the course of six months and around six meetings, the relationship became one of the strongest I had among all of my clients. I was invited to the company's business events, to join industry groups they ran, to work with their sales and marketing teams (something only key partners were invited to do). I used the entire sales process to turn this relationship around, but a vital foundation was rapport. We must always act to strengthen rapport and our relationships.

This is the last area we'll cover before getting into the specific stages of the sales process: building rapport. Rapport is fundamental when working with patients, which is why it's at the centre of the model. It's necessary throughout every stage. Once you've engaged your patient (and even before that, depending on the situation), you must develop rapport and trust. This will ensure the working relationship between you and your patient is built on a solid foundation.

How do we build rapport?

There are many perspectives on rapport, but I see it as the ability to relate to others in a way that creates a level of trust and understanding. Rapport helps build a relaxed, positive relationship. In consultative selling interactions, it enables the patient and the dental professional to unconsciously gain agreement and acceptance.

So how do we go about creating it? Here are a few ways to build rapport with patients (as well as with friends, family and colleagues):

- Smile (we'll talk about the flooding smile in the next section)
- Use body language to show openness, trust and understanding
- Be interested – ask genuine questions about the person and their situation
- Make eye contact, especially when the other person is talking

- Listen actively by leaning in and acknowledging what they're saying
- Be grateful and respectful
- Enjoy spending time with them (make a conscious effort to do so)
- Create common ground
- Build trust over time by showing genuine empathy, being present and engaged in all interactions, and doing what you say you'll do

Emotional bank accounts

When I became a business manager, an experienced colleague of mine (let's call him Jon) taught me about the idea of an emotional bank account. I later learned that this principle is from The 7 Habits of Highly Effective People, by Stephen Covey.[20] The principle works the same way as a traditional bank account. To have a positive balance, you need to make deposits into the account.

If you make too many withdrawals, you'll be overdrawn. Jon ensured that he provided his sales team with support, praise, reassurance, and encouragement – all were deposits in their Emotional Bank Accounts. Sometimes he'd make short-notice requests of his team, which would constitute a withdrawal from their Emotional Bank Accounts, but he continually invested in his team so that the balance remained positive.

20 S Covey, The 7 Habits of Highly Effective People (Simon and Schuster, 1989)

Keep this principle in mind to maintain a positive relationship with your patients. All the small deposits you make will positively impact your patient – for example, you and your team always do what you say you'll do when you say you'll do it. Here are a few other ideas, capture personal information about your patients and log them in the Patient Management Software, then familiarise yourself with their records before an appointment, they will see you remembering their family, their role, their holidays, birthdays, and other significant events. Be interested and ask about these things.

Speak with your team and ensure everyone working on the practice is courteous and respectful. Consider other patients who have similar treatments, share the outcomes and impact those other patients have experienced, at the right time this will reassure them when making decisions.

Finally, make sure you're giving them space and time during appointments, so they don't feel rushed. There are lots of ways to make positive deposits, the more you consider them, the bigger the positive impact you and your team can make. By investing in your patients this way, you'll also be able to make requests of them when needed (but only when the balance of the 'account' is positive).

If you keep this principle in mind with your patients, they will move heaven and earth for you. This is a way to build lifelong loyalty and for your practice and business to continually grow.

Consultative Sales Mastery: Deepening rapport and using emotions

Using your face, body language and voice

In her book How to Talk to Anyone, Leil Lowndes explains several ways (ninety-two, in fact) to create rapport and strengthen relationships.[7] The one that is most relevant to deepening our learning about rapport in this chapter is the flooding smile.

The flooding smile

The technique for flooding smiles is to wait before smiling at the recipient instead of smiling straight away. Look at the person's face for a moment, soak in their persona and then give them a warm, broad smile in response. The evidence suggests that the recipient of this smile will feel as though it's special and just for them, so unconsciously, it will mean more to them. If someone sees us smiling when we see them, the smile wasn't especially for us. This is a great start to building rapport!

Matching and mirroring

Isn't it interesting how you can watch people talking in a café or restaurant and be able to tell whether or not they're getting along? Body language gives it away. If they have rapport, they'll be unconsciously copying each other's

7 L Lowndes, How to Talk to Anyone: 92 little tricks for big success in relationships (HarperElement, 2014)

positions, actions and movements. You can do this consciously with your patients. By gradually matching and mirroring your patient's body position, arm and hand gestures, posture and distance (leaning in or away), you'll deepen your rapport. With practice, you can increase the speed with which you build rapport with almost anyone. You can even try it at a distance with people you want to engage or influence. Try it and see! Once you've built deep rapport, you can then lead the rapport with your patient – you'll move, and they'll follow.

Voice

How you say something is just as important as what you say. The way in which we speak – pace, tone and language patterns – allows us to engage other people and strengthen rapport. Your job at the outset is to reflect your patient's pace and tone so that you're 'harmonising' with them. Then listen to the language they're using.

You don't have to copy it exactly but notice it and use similar patterns. When we spend time with people we like, we start to pick up their words and expressions. You can make a conscious effort to do this with patients. Your rapport will become stronger, and your patience may even start to use some of your language – the ultimate compliment in rapport!

Remember: rapport is unconscious and reciprocal. If you enjoy an interaction, your patient will be drawn to enjoy it too (without even realising it).

Handling the breakdown of rapport

When we're under pressure, we may stop acting naturally and start trying to force ourselves to act differently. As rapport (or loss of it) is unconscious, the other person will instinctively notice a disconnect. You might be able to recall situations where you felt this disconnect yourself, whether it was with a patient or when you were a customer or in the company of someone who made you uncomfortable. Once you notice this disconnect, you can re-establish rapport by following these simple steps:

1. Put yourself and the other person at ease by making a light joke or pointing out a distraction you can both focus on.

2. Regain genuine interest in the person. You might apologise for taking the conversation off track and then ask an open question. For example: 'Sorry, I had to point that out. It was just so interesting. Anyway, you were telling me about your plans for later in the year. How are they looking so far?'
3. Listen intently and generate empathy for the other person.
4. Lean in and show your interest.
5. Ask simple, expansive questions (you might be surprised by how effectively these keep a conversation flowing): Wow, tell me more about that.
6. What else happened?
7. What happened next?
8. How did that make you feel?

9. Once the conversation flows again, match the other person's body language and you'll notice you're back on track.

It really can be this simple. With practice, it will become easier and easier to build and strengthen your rapport, even with the most difficult people.

A different perspective on rapport

Think about how easy it is to spend time with close friends and family. In a relaxed environment, with no pressure, you're likely using some, if not all, of the techniques in this section about rapport without realising it. Now that you're aware, you can consciously improve your rapport-building skills.

In Chapters 3 and 4 we looked at visualising a positive outcome. Visualisation will also prime you to naturally generate the kind of rapport you need with your patients. When it comes to building rapport with patients you may find difficult, try this visualisation technique.

EXERCISE: AMONG FRIENDS

1. Imagine you're catching up with a close friend over a drink or dinner.
2. Notice the way you interact with each other – how easy it is and how relaxed you both are.
3. Think about what you see, what you hear and what you feel.
4. Now imagine the patient sitting with you and your friend.

5. Imagine them joining the discussion and enjoying the time with you and your friend.
6. Notice how this changes your perception of them.

After completing this exercise, you'll likely notice a difference in the way you think/feel about and act towards this patient. Answer these questions in your journal or notebook:

- What have I learned?
- What if I commit to learning?
- What will my patient and I gain as a result?

If you want to learn more, there are plenty of books on rapport, body language and relationship building.[8] This subject is fascinating, and it's worth investing your time in it.

Rapport – a counter note

There may be times when you don't want to build rapport – maybe someone has annoyed you or you want to end a conversation or you're the subject of unwanted attention. You can consciously break rapport by doing the opposite of everything recommended in this chapter so far. Remember, rapport is unconscious. If you consciously break it, the other person will feel uncomfortable and, unless they're a self-obsessed megalomaniac, find it hard to stick around. The quickest way to break rapport is to:

- Avoid eye contact

8 Two things I recommend as a great place to start are: D Carnegie, How to Win Friends and Influence People (Vermilion, 2006), and J Borg, Body Language: How to know what's really being said, third edition (Pearson, 2013)

- Fold your arms (use 'closed' body language)
- Don't ask any questions
- Don't show any interest in them
- Turn your body away from them and look to engage someone else

Using emotions

This might sound like an odd topic to include in a book about consultative communication and sales, but most purchase decisions are based on emotion, not logic. Many patients (and people in general) will believe they're buying based on logic and will have objective reasons to support their buying decisions. When you're discussing treatment options or dental plans with your patient, keep in mind that everyone buys to satisfy their feelings – feelings associated with the product/service, the company and the dental professional. To be more consistently successful when you're having those conversations, tap into emotions and evoke powerful feelings in your patient. To do so, it's important to establish three fundamentals in your patient relationship:

- Trust – you do what you say you'll do (to satisfy your patient)
- Confidence – you have the experience and abilities (you're their best choice).
- Support – you have concern for their needs (during and after the treatment/ plan starts)

As you learn about the INSPIRe Consultative Sales System, you'll see how you can leverage the power of emotions to better serve your patients and ensure your success in meeting their needs. Your ability to question your patients and position your solutions according to their needs will set you and your organisation apart from other providers. Whatever you're discussing with your patients, consider these questions, which will help you tap into the positive emotions of your patients. Capture your answers in your journal or notebook.

- What is the greatest positive impact working with me will have on my patient?
- What is the greatest obstacle I can enable my patients to overcome?
- How grateful will my patient be for my support?
- How far and wide is the impact of this treatment on my patients and their relationships, confidence and their life?
- What are the words and feelings my patient would use to express their gratitude?

Reflect on your answers to these questions, as they'll help you tap into the motivation you need to stay connected to your patient's emotions. This in turn will help you to meet their needs more effectively. Remember, people buy on emotions, in an effort to satisfy their feelings, then they justify with logic. Not the other way round. By helping them do this, you're meeting their needs beyond the consultative conversation.

Before we move on, reflect on this chapter and write down your thoughts in your journal or notebook.

OPTIONAL EXERCISE: BUILDING RAPPORT

Look for opportunities to practise intentional deepening of rapport. It may be with someone you don't get on with well; it may be at social gatherings or with work colleagues. Start to notice what happens when you develop rapport and how you can lead the other person in actions and conversation.

When you've gained confidence, try and tackle more difficult people with this approach of "rapport first". Think of someone with whom it has been challenging for you to connect and try using your rapport-deepening skills and practices. You'll be surprised at how you can win these people over and gain a deeper connection with them when you take this approach.

PART THREE

THE SALES SYSTEM

Chapter 8: Insight And Impact

Insight & Impact Maxim:
"Not standing out is the same as being invisible."

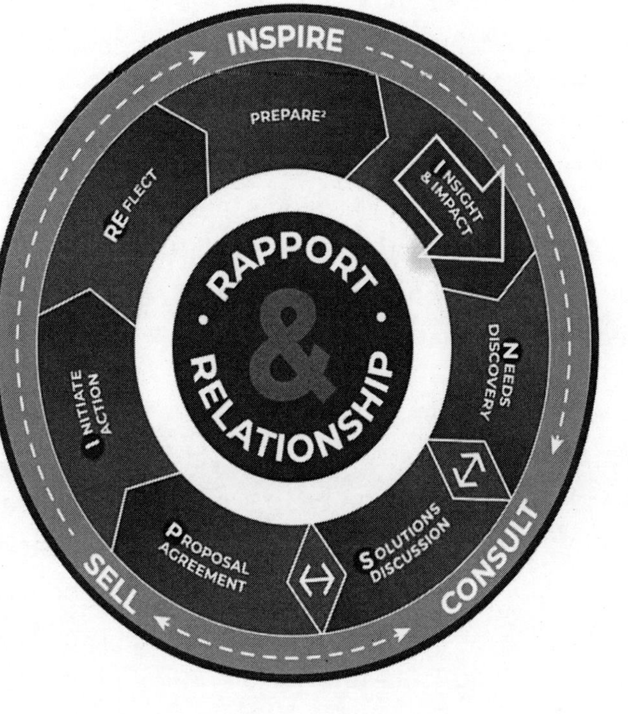

INSPIRe – Consultative Sales System: Insight and Impact

At the second dental company I worked for, I had a sales colleague who was confident, experienced and funny (we'll call him Roger). He joined the company shortly after I did and was new to the dental industry. After he'd been with the company for about six months, he was accompanied by the managing director (MD) on a 'dual calling' field sales day. These types of accompanying days can be quite nerve-wracking it's like being under supervision by patients, the pressure gets turned up. On their first call together to a new dental practice, Roger and the MD were met with a frosty receptionist whose body language made it clear she wasn't impressed that their hand turned up unannounced.

Sensing the cold front, Roger made a bold decision. He put on a serious face and said, 'Good morning, we're from Her Majesty's Revenue and Customs, and we're here to see Dr Bannister to inspect his books.' Well, the receptionist went white with shock! She explained that Dr Bannister had a full patient list and that this would wreak havoc on their work that day, and so on, and so on.

Roger then let a large smile creep across his face and said, 'How pleased would you be to see a couple of dental reps right now?' The receptionist fell back in her chair and smiled with relief. She called Roger a 'cheeky devil' and asked him to take a seat, saying, 'I'll fit you in when I can.' Roger and the MD made quite an impression on both the receptionist and the dentist, who also found Roger's introduction hilarious. The story became legendary in the company and the industry, and so did Roger.

Now I'm not suggesting that you tell your patients you're working for Inland revenue and want to check their taxes. This approach was a huge risk that might not have paid off, but it does illustrate a couple of important points about first impressions. The first is that it's important to make a memorable first impression, and the second is that you can use humour to disarm people.

Let's look more closely at first impressions before we dive into the sales process.

First impressions

You've probably heard the saying 'you only get one chance to make a good first impression'. Well, it's absolutely true. Research suggests that most people make a judgment about someone within seven seconds of meeting them.[9] While it's possible to get a relationship back on track if the first impression isn't good, a not-so-great first impression takes time to correct. Why leave it to chance? It's important to get it right.

In his brilliant book 'How to Win Friends and Influence People', Dale Carnegie outlines several ways to create bonds with people quickly. If you haven't read it, I recommend it. One of Carnegie's suggestions is to consciously use a person's name over and over, in an appropriate way. This helps you and the other person to become familiar with each other and creates a connection.[10]

9 'First Impressions', Psychology Today, no date, www.psychologytoday. com/intl/basics/first-impressions, accessed 28 September 2020 10 D Carnegie, How to Win Friends and Influence People (Vermilion, 2006)

A persons' name is one of the single most important word in their own language, using it intentionally and early in a relationship can deepen a connection more quickly. This is effective in all kinds of situations. When you're at an event meeting new people or in a restaurant, noticing the other person's name and then using it will make a positive impression on them. It could help you build a stronger professional network and get better service or preferential treatment. Try it for yourself and see.

Humour

Using humour appropriately can help you build patient relationships. You can use the INSPIRe Consultative Sales System to amplify your sense of humour, uniqueness, and personality. Once you're confident that you have the structure in place, your own humour becomes a valuable complement to the process you're using. One-liners, funny stories, well-timed jokes and/or anecdotes are an important part of being yourself with your patients. Once you relax and use the process, you can use humour as you would with family and friends to engage your patient. You can increasingly 'be yourself' and let your sense of humour shine through – whatever that means for you. Just make sure you always keep things professional and appropriate, it's important to keep in mind when we're building lifelong loyal patient relationships.

One study looked specifically at the use of humour to get customers to pay more. They found that when customers were engaged using jokes and humour, they were willing to pay a higher price![11] It seems you can put a price on laughter.

Introducing yourself to new patients

Have you ever experienced someone introducing themselves to you and you had to ask them to repeat themselves because they spoke so fast you couldn't catch what they said? It's a common occurrence, we naturally become so familiar with our own name and experience we forget we need to slow down for new patients or for patients who haven't seen us for 6 months. Here's some useful guidance on introducing yourself during a new patient consultation and perhaps for reintroducing ourselves.

- Be clear on what you'll say and how you'll say it. Ask yourself, 'How would I want someone to introduce themselves to me if I were a new patient?'
- Speak clearly, concisely and positively.
- Ensure that your introduction is warm and friendly – and smile (even if you're on the phone).
- Introduce yourself and any of your team who are working with you.
- Say your patient's name, tell them it's nice to see them and make them as welcome and comfortable as possible.

11 K O'Quin and J Aronoff, 'Humor as a technique for social influence', Social Psychology Quarterly, 44/4 (1981), 349–357

This is a fundamental first principle of influence. We must connect with the patient and introduce (or reintroduce) ourselves and our team at every appointment. It immediately reassures and relaxes the patient, even if they're a confident patient, getting into this habit will strengthen your connection and influencing ability.

Now that you've made your first impression, you're ready to create value. It's time to explore insight and impact.

Generate and tailor

Insight is information that's directly relevant to your patient. The idea is to research and discover facts, data and/or opinions that aren't common knowledge but could be incredibly valuable to your patient. Once you've uncovered your insights, tailor it to your patient and the potential treatment option so that it has a positive impact on them (i.e., it's meaningful to them).

Insight and impact can take many forms, depending on the treatment option and your patient. To generate insight, consider reviewing the following:

- The dental marketplace (trends, data, future direction & innovation)
- The 'consumer' dental marketplace (feedback, opinions, demographics)
- Dental Influencers, Key Opinion Leaders & Thought Leaders (best practices, successes, new evidence, new interpretations)

- A little known or hidden opportunity or risk (white papers, care pathways, whole-life costs, financial options, misinformation, etc.)

You'll have noticed that in the early stages of this book I included a section titled "Five Vital Insights for dental professionals". These insights are an example of this stage in our process. They're a combination of data from the wider marketplace, the dental market, guidance from the GDC and combined they share powerful knowledge. They bring together many different factors that are driving growth and for many people who learn about them for the first time, they can be disruptive to their point of view. That's exactly the point of them.

The idea is to share knowledge, join up the dots and ensure that insights come together to have a positive and often disruptive effect on the other person. When I'm teaching about Consultative communication and selling, I have a series of insights I use to help clients understand the value of training. When discussing a programme about coaching as a leadership style, I have a different series of insights I share with clients. When I'm discussing leadership training for boards of directors, I have yet another series of insights I share and questions I ask.

This is an opportunity for you to develop a series of insights about each of the specialist treatment areas you offer to your patients. Whatever your preferred treatment areas, orthodontics, veneers, cosmetic treatments, implantology, prosthodontics, etc… Your potential for greater impact for your patients comes from learning beyond the treatment option and extends to the relevant wider marketplace.

Make notes on your worksheet:

- What treatment options are in your specialist interest areas?
- What insights should you research and gather?
- What might you include in your impact statement for each treatment?

This will create a template you can use when engaging your patient in the early stages of your relationship or when a patient is considering a new treatment option. Here's the link to the worksheet again:

https://bit.ly/INSPIRe-Worksheet-ICS

You can revisit this tool whenever you need to look for insight and create impact statements. They're useful for all treatment options, but vital when offering new treatment options or patient services.

Consultative Sales Mastery: Make yourself invaluable

As you develop your skills in this area, learn to continually research the field most relevant to your patients. Start to look into the future and not at the past or present. Learn from the thought leaders in your field. Learn what they are predicting will happen and share these insights with your patients. Start to see yourself as someone who is continually starting each patient interaction with insight and impact. However long you've been seeing your patients, use this approach to make sure the relationship is of continual value to your patient.

When you master this approach and it becomes part of your ongoing discussions with your patients, they will start to see you as a valuable resource and as someone who is invested in their oral health and their wellbeing. When you develop this level of trust with your patients, your opinions and recommendations become more valuable, and price becomes less of an obstacle in any treatment discussion.

So, you're in a treatment discussion with a patient. You engage them through your insights and share them in a way that's positively impactful. They're now keen to learn more about how they can benefit from what you've explained so far. You're in a strong position of potential influence. What comes next is a step in a different direction for most people. The next step is where the magic happens.

Before we move on, reflect on this chapter and write down your thoughts in your journal or notebook.

OPTIONAL EXERCISE: SHARING THE IMPACT STATEMENT

This practical exercise is one I use with clients and is designed to be practised with a colleague (preferably someone who also wants to practise their consultative sales technique).

Use your client scenario from Chapter 6 (the challenging patient you've identified). Decide who will be the patient and who will be the dental professional. The dental professional will then brief the patient on the scenario, explain the challenges the patient presents and what your plan is to handle the consultation.

Practise delivering your introduction and impact statement.

Discuss with your colleague how this sounds. Keep practicing until it delivers sounds and feels natural to you. Ask your colleague to tell you too. How impactful is it?

Keep working on it until you create an impact statement that gives you what you need to engage your patients and kickstart your consultative treatment discussion and sales process.

Chapter 9: Needs Discovery

Needs Maxim:

"Everything you need to convince your patient is in their head."

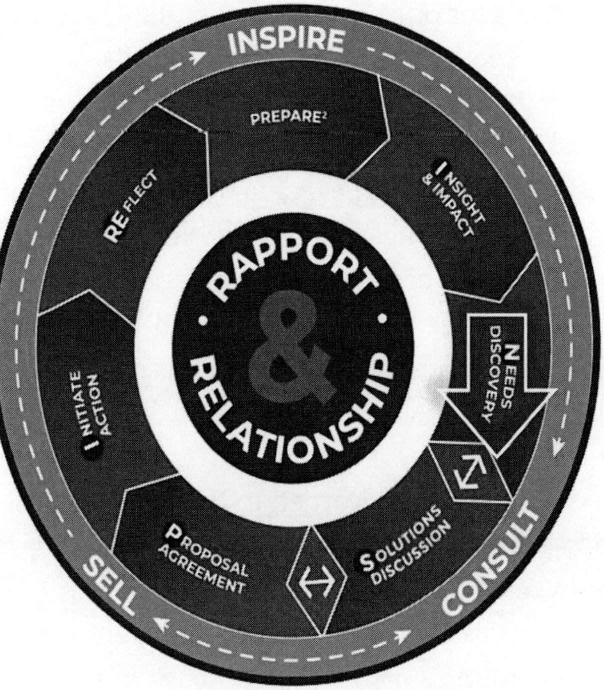

INSPIRe – Consultative Sales System: Needs Discovery

In 2003 whilst I was working as a Key Account Manager, I was responsible for Key distributors in the dental market and the corporate dental groups that were becoming more influential. I had another member of the team working with me to support the sales and marketing activity, they had secured a meeting and asked me to join them.

The client meeting was in London and the client was a senior dentist working in one of the emerging dental corporates (we'll call him Pete). We were meeting to discuss how we might better support him in his work while exploring opportunities for our portfolio across the group. Pete was a highly experienced dentist who felt 'disenchanted' (his words) by the work he'd been doing so far. He felt powerless and frustrated by the non-clinical workload alongside his clinical practice. My colleague asked Pete questions about his priorities and long-term aspirations, and Pete's answers were incredibly negative. To be honest, it was quite depressing! I was studying NLP and was beginning to understand its potential. I was interested in Pete's body language, emotional state and verbal language. Having a sense that there was a way to turn the meeting around, I recalled something I'd learned in the NLP studies. It was a question I repeated to myself when I was feeling stumped, lost or in need of inspiration, and I still use it to this day. What is the best question I can ask right now? It's an invaluable prompt for creating a change in my own mental state and others'.

I looked at Pete and my colleague and asked, "Do you mind if I ask a question?" My colleague looked relieved (this is a useful way to change a subject or create a change in a conversation – simply ask permission to do so, and you'll rarely get declined).

'Pete, what's been your greatest achievement in the last twelve months? What are you most proud of?'

He looked surprised then quickly said, 'I'm not sure there is anything, it's been a tough year."

'So, you're telling me that in the whole of the last year, there isn't anything you've achieved at work that you're proud of?'

This seemed to shock him again. There was a silence while he thought long and hard. I signalled to my colleague to stay quiet. Finally, Pete said, 'Well, there's the CPD programme we put in place this year."

I feigned a look of surprise. A CPD programme? Tell me more about that.'

He went on to tell us about the project he'd led – a company-wide CPD programme covering clinical and non-clinical skills to train their entire clinical team across the group. He explained how he'd coordinated a significant piece of work to build an entire programme that was tailored to the group's business plan. He'd secured investment to build the content and engaged leading clinicians within the group to run the sessions. They'd begun the roll out of the training and the feedback had been incredible. It was an impressive achievement, but one Pete had overlooked as being important at all.

The meeting transformed. Once Pete had tapped into the positive event and was explaining it and experiencing it again, everything changed – his posture, his body language, his attitude. Everything. My colleague and I were genuinely impressed and complimented him on leading such a significant programme. We ended up uncovering a significant opportunity that complemented his recent work and would deliver benefits to his team and improve future patient treatment. In that same meeting, we secured a follow-up meeting with him and his finance team to make sure that our product evaluation would get the right support from the outset (an important lesson he'd learned from the CPD programme). This account became a significant customer for our business.

It is possible to turn around difficult patient discussions (and team member discussions). When you ask the right questions, you can help your patients in ways they don't realise are possible. You can create opportunities that have benefits that are far reaching for your patients, for you and for the profession in which you practice. Your potential in a professional role goes far beyond success in dentistry. If you want to, you can make a real difference in the world.

Resist the urge to pitch

So, back to our consultative communication and sales system. You've made it past first base and established a positive connection with the patient, they're engaged. You've delivered a powerful impact statement and they're interested in hearing more.

This is where it's really tempting to jump into "pitching". Tell the patient what's so great about your practice, your team, the treatment options, your experience, the features of the treatment and how it's going to help them, etc....

STOP, don't do it!

In my experience, when relationships between dental professionals and patients are at risk, this is the moment. After a strong positive start, you need to build on that momentum with 'Needs Discovery' which you can only do through questioning and listening. This is arguably the most important stage of the system for a number of reasons.

It will:

- Build the foundation for your treatment solution discussion
- Unlock your patient's priorities, challenges and needs
- Gives you a window into your patient's world
- Strengthen your rapport with the patient
- Show you what your patient thinks
- Help you understand what your patients like and, importantly, what they don't like
- Help you identify the best way to position your solution (and how not to)
- Enable you to better understand how you can truly satisfy your patience

The challenge at this stage is that it can feel as if you're delaying because it falls to the patient to do most of the talking. But don't be fooled. You're not delaying – you're learning. Enjoy this part of the process. It is, without a doubt, one of the most valuable investments of time you can make in your patient consultation. You may have heard the expression 'You have two ears and one mouth so that you can listen twice as much as you speak'. This is particularly relevant during this part of our process. This is the time to learn our patients' motivations, needs and reasons to move forward with treatment.

In Chapter 1, we looked at the three important components of your client proposition. Here's a recap. Remember, they'll be assessing and questioning:
1 – The Person (you the clinician)
2 – The Practice (your organisation)
3 – The Products (the treatment options)

This is the ideal time to learn exactly what your patient is looking for from you, from the treatment option and from your organisation. Find out as much as you can about them and their needs. You can do this only by questioning, listening and responding.

We'll walk through each of these one at a time.

Before we start with questioning and listening, we may have intrigued the patient to such an extent that they might be so keen to hear about the treatment that they ask you to continue. If this happens, simply say "I'd love to tell you more about the treatment, but before I do would it be OK if I asked you a few questions to make sure I recommend the most appropriate option for you?" By adding this immediately after your impact statement, you're creating a natural segue into the Need Discovery stage. You can now ask whichever questions will be most beneficial for you and your patient, so you can make a more informed recommendation.

Questioning (high-quality questions)

It's a fact: not all questions are created equal. There's a clear distinction between high-quality questions (HQQs) and all other questions. While it may not be possible to ask HQQs all the time, you should strive to do so as often as possible in your patient interactions. You'll see a number of examples in this chapter and will also get the chance to create a few of your own. Once you've worked through the exercises and identified the HQQs that you think will produce the best results for you, you can improve your patient consultations significantly.

HQQs will put you on a fast track to learning about your patients' dreams, emotions and current and future needs, challenges and priorities. You can naturally build on these questions, and they'll unlock information you may not have believed you could get from your patients.

HQQs generally fall into one of three categories:

- Open
- Closed
- Probing

All three are useful throughout the consultative discussion and within our sales system, but they're particularly important in the Needs Discovery stage. The key is to understand when to ask each type of question and to become more aware of the questions you currently ask. As a guide, you will ask Open questions early on in the discussion, probing questions throughout and closing questions as you near the end of the patient discussion and are seeking feedback and commitment. Let's look at each type more closely.

Open questions

This is the most useful in terms of getting your patients talking and opening up to you. They are expansive questions that help you to gain a greater understanding – they encourage people to respond with information, creating conversational flow.

There are lots of different open questions, but the simplest way to ask an Open question is to remember:

- What
- How
- Who
- Where

- When
- Why (only in reverse)

Start using 'what' or 'how' at the beginning of any question you ask, and you will have created an effective open question. These words will help you elicit more information from your patient (or anyone else) than almost all others. Once you form the habit of starting your HQQs with 'what' or 'how', you'll open up a new world of information. Quiet people will become talkers – the secret lies in the questions you ask. If you're finding that certain patients 'dry up' on you, master open questions. You'll give your patients consultations a new lease of life. Plan your open questions in advance to make them even more powerful.

'Who' is also useful when you want to understand other decision makers and their influence, and when you're interested in the people whose opinion matters to your patient (their partner, family, friends, network, peers, etc.).

'Who', 'where' and 'when' can be used to generate clarifying open questions, when you need to be clear on your patient's decision-making criteria or cycle, the other people involved and the best way to move forward. For example:

- Who else should I include in the confirmation email?
- Where is the best place to send the details?
- When are you planning to make the final decision?

While these words will create an open question, they won't open up your patient discussions the way that 'what' and 'how' will.

A note about 'why'

'Why' allows you to dig deep – fast! It's personal and powerful. But when using 'why', you must take great care. Many people are hard-wired to react defensively when asked a 'why' question. One reason is that in childhood we are very often asked 'why' questions in an aggressive way by adults when we're suspected of doing something wrong, whether we have or not. We learn to become defensive in the light of a 'why' question. We must take care when asking 'why' questions because it can:

- Seems like an accusation and makes your patient uncomfortable
- Be misinterpreted as a negatively positioned question
- Create distance between you and the patient
- Evoke strong negative emotions in your patient
- Cause your patients to get defensive about themselves or their decisions
- Interfere with the rapport you've built

A good principle to follow if you want to use a 'why' question is to use it in reverse or to discover your patient's passion. This means using it when you want your patient to defend or compliment you, or if you want them to speak more deeply about their own desires or passions. These questions work best when rapport is strong, the patient is onside, and you are confident there is good potential for acceptance of the treatment option.

The why questions could be structured like this.

To encourage the patient to compliment you:

- Why would you choose to have this treatment with us?
- Why do you think treatment with us would be your best option?
- Why do you think we're worthy of a recommendation?

To unlock the patient's desires and passions:

- Why is it important that you get the result you're looking for?
- Why do you think this will make such an impact for you?
- Why is investing in yourself this way so important to you?
- Why does this transformation mean so much to you?

You can see that these 'why' questions will elicit a positive emotional response, one that will increase the closeness of your relationship with your patient.

Objective questions

You can use 'what' or 'how' in place of 'why' to make your questions more objective. If, for example, you ask your patient, 'Why haven't you had this treatment before now' they'll likely feel as if they need to defend their decision or delay and it might even make them reconsider. If instead you ask, 'How did you decide that now was the right time for treatment?' or 'What things did you consider when you were making the decision to go ahead with the treatment?' you seem more objective and are likely to gather information much more freely from your patients.

High-quality questions bank

Here are some examples of HQQs that will help you unlock your patient's needs, motivations, challenges and priorities. The list isn't exhaustive but will give you some good ideas for your patient consultations.

- Where do you see your oral health in five years?
- How would you describe your smile?
- How would you like to describe your smile?
- What is your highest priority for treatment?
- What are your main considerations for the treatment?
- What is your greatest reservation?
- What would you like me to do to reassure you?
- What could get in the way of your plans?
- What are your three biggest challenges/ priorities for treatment?
- What are the big decisions you'll have to make about treatment?
- How do you think you'll make those decisions?

- Who is helping and supporting you as you make them?
- Who else will you involve in making the decision for treatment?
- What have you found most difficult?
- If we had to choose one thing to focus on for the treatment, what would it be?
- How would you like to be communicated with as a patient throughout treatment?
- What would you advise me to do to improve our service to you?
- If you were me, what else would you ask?
- What have I missed?
- How confident are you about the treatment plan?
- Which is more important to you, quality or price?
- *If you could change one thing, what would it be?*

(More on this one later in the chapter.)

You can find a document containing the high-quality questions here: https://bit.ly/HQQ-BANK-ICS. We call it HQQ Bank. It also includes space for you to create your own HQQs. This bank will give you a strong foundation for questioning and should stimulate your thinking about how to develop your questioning skills.

Now let's get practical. Think about your situation, your patients, your business and your treatment options. Then create several of your own high-quality (open) questions (using 'what', 'how' and 'who') that would help you better understand your patients' needs, motivations and decision-making.

In your journal or notebook, write down ten questions starting with 'what' and 'how'. These example questions will be a useful guide before patient meetings.

Closed questions

The answer to a closed question is either 'yes' or 'no'. The only times you should use closed questions in your patient meetings is when you're:

- Clarifying or checking an answer (Did you mean this?)
- Confirming information (I have this written down – is that right?)
- Making a commitment to move forward (Would you be happy to proceed with treatment?)

In these circumstances, it's valuable to use closed questions. Any other time, they will shut down your patient conversations, stifle your consultations and even create difficult silences. As a coach and mentor, I continue to be surprised by the number of closed questions people use. Unfortunately, they seem to come more naturally to us than open questions. But if you're someone who asks a lot of closed questions, don't worry – with awareness and practice, you can easily change this behaviour. The impact is truly transformational.

Reflect on your own questioning skills. If you find yourself in situations where your patients or friends stop talking or answer 'yes' or 'no', you're asking closed questions.

Closed questions will start with these words:

- Have
- Will
- Can
- Do
- Did
- Are
- Is

Remember, closed questions have their place, but you must use them at the right time – not when you're trying to 'open up' a conversation or person you're speaking with.

Consider the structure of these questions and the different types of answers they would elicit from you or your patients:

- 'Are you OK?' versus 'How are you?'
- 'Can I make an appointment?' versus 'What would be the best way to make an appointment?'
- 'Do you have any feedback on the treatment plan?' versus 'What are your thoughts on the treatment plan?'
- 'Do you like your smile?' versus 'How would you improve your smile?'
- 'Anything else?' versus 'What else?'

Notice how similar the questions sound but how different the answers to them would be.

Make a note in your journal or notebook about how you'll remind yourself to distinguish between open and closed questions and when you need to use them. Remember the golden rule – 'What' or 'How' are open questions.

Probing questions

Probing questions can be either open or closed, but they'll allow you to gain further information: information that many other dental professionals might not ask for. Probing allows you to fully understand the specific needs of your patient and delve deeper into the important parts of their world – in particular, their priorities, emotions and challenges. Probing is about not taking things at face value. Sometimes you get a sense that there's more to your patient than they're telling you. This is when it's appropriate to probe. A lot of dental professionals are so keen to get to the next consultation or appointment that they don't take the time to really understand their patients. This is what probing will allow you to do.

Probing questions can be simple and take different forms. The key when probing is to be genuinely interested, lean in and use one or both of these phrases in turn:

- Please, tell me more.
- What else is important?

These two simple phrases are well known to evoke deeper thoughts and are used widely in coaching. Used in consultations, they will help you gain more insight and a deeper connection with your patients and their needs.
In your journal or notebook, describe how you intend to use these in your patient consultations and team interactions.

The magic question

Patients and team members can sometimes be resistant to change and finding a way to get them to see beyond their current position or ways of thinking and acting can be difficult. But when you're trying to get patients to consider improvements to their smile or oral function, you have a powerful tool at your disposal – this question:

> *If you could change one thing about your smile/ oral health/ dentition, what would it be?*

This question will stimulate your patient's thinking. It's rare to encounter a situation where the patient wouldn't change one thing. Once they tell you that 'one thing', get them committed to changing it. You can do that by probing. Remember, it's about digging deep and truly understanding the patient's issue or priority and how much value there is for them in solving it.

The structure of this question is also worth reviewing. It's a presupposition – in other words, a presumption of information or facts. The positioning of the question makes an assumption that there is one thing the patient would change.

This question does several things:
It takes the patient forward; beyond the decision they're making.

- It connects you to their clarity of something they'd like to change.
- It helps them to get clear on their priorities for potential treatment.
- It gives you higher-quality information and feedback.
- It strengthens the patient's buy-in to you and your capabilities.
- It creates a real win-win scenario!

A third-party perspective

Sometimes, your patient just won't play ball, even if you're asking HQQs. They won't commit to an answer, and they won't admit that they have an issue or a need. In these situations, it can be useful to share a third-party perspective. Simply put, tell them about other patients that have had this specific issue or need and overcome it. In my experience, this seems to relieve the pressure on the patient. Up to that point, they might have felt that they had to admit to something they are ashamed of or something they should already have resolved. As soon as you move the issue or need another patient, your patient might find it easier to admit that they're experiencing the same thing. This simple statement can unlock a defensive or resistant patient: 'Yes, a number of patients have approached me with this same issue, and they were surprised by how easily we were able to help them resolve it.'

Once your patient admits to having the same issue, ask questions. You need to understand how it affects them personally.

Listen, take notes and summarise

Learning to listen

Remember that expression 'You have two ears and one mouth so that you can listen twice as much as you speak'? It's worth repeating here. It's a good way to remember just how important listening is in your patient interactions. Listening is a learned skill, and it's not as easy as it sounds. In long patient consultations, it can be a challenge to stay focused on listening. But when you ask HQQs, you must listen, consciously and intently, to your patient's answers. If you don't, there's no point asking questions.

As with any skill or development area, we can improve our listening skills through awareness, a desire to change, and practice. Here are some examples of the blocks to listening that you may or may not be aware of:

- Presuming or mind reading (guessing what will be said next)
- Filtering (leaving out pieces of information)

- Waiting to speak (having your response or next question ready)
- Mind wandering (losing track of the conversation, getting distracted)
- Bringing it back to yourself (taking in everything that was said and then referencing your own experience)
- Interrupting the speaker (not allowing the patient to finish)
- Changing the subject (directing the conversation towards a topic you want to discuss)
- Being impatient (showing your irritation)
- Overemphasizing (listening too actively, so that it becomes insincere)

You may know people who display these listening blocks, or you may display them yourself. To improve your listening skills, you must be self-aware, so take a moment to reflect on your own blocks when it comes to listening to your patients.

What do you need to work on most? Write them down in your journal or notebook.

A well-recognised model – described particularly well in the book Co-Active Coaching, by Henry Kimsey- House, Karen Kimsey-House and Phillip Sandahl[13] – defines three levels of listening that can help you become a more active listener.

Here's my interpretation:

Level 1 – Internal listening (conversational): Listening while waiting to speak

- Your own inner voice is commentating
- Giving your own opinion and sharing stories

Level 2 – Listening to understand (one-way): Completely focused on your patient

- Only asking questions that are relevant to them
- Listening to truly deepen understanding
- Speaking only to clarify or reflect what you've heard

Level 3 – Global Listening (beyond the words): Listening to more than just the words that are said

- Noticing body language
- Listening for tonality and accentuation of words
- Sensing energy levels, feelings and emotions
- Trusting your instincts to guide your responses and questions

When you are in consultation with your patients you may start your conversation with level 1 listening. Once you have started the Needs Discovery stage it's critical to consciously listen at levels 2 and 3 – this will require a concerted effort.

13 H Kimsey-House, K Kimsey-House and P Sandahl, Co-Active Coaching: The proven framework for transformative conversations at work and in life, fourth edition (Aladdin, 2018)

Here are my top five tips to improve your listening and more consistently listen at levels 2 and 3:

1. Set yourself a 'level 2 and 3 listening challenge' before each patient discussion.
2. Use the techniques we looked at in the section for 'Deepening rapport and using emotions'.
3. Now, lean in and mirror your patient's body language (be interested and show it).
4. Reflect, repeat and paraphrase the key words your patient uses.
5. Notice, acknowledge and silence your own inner voice.

Repeating & Paraphrasing

It's important to repeat key words that your patient uses. In doing so, you're acknowledging that you're listening and also reinforcing on an unconscious level that you truly understand what the patient is telling you. Once you deliberately set out to repeat your patient's words and paraphrase what they've said, you'll be compelled to listen more actively. The more you do it, the better you'll get – and this skill will improve many areas of your life. Start practising with everyone you meet from now on.

There is a direct link between listening and body language. It's worth rereading the section in Chapter 7 on body language.

The power of silence

It may seem obvious, but to listen, you must be silent. This is not as easy as it sounds. Many of us have negative associations with silence, perhaps because of childhood experiences in schools, museums or churches or time spent with older relatives. We can also find silence uncomfortable, especially if we spend a lot of time with people who like to talk. For some, there is only silence when they sleep! But if you can become more aware of silence and when to use it, you'll be granted greater insight into your relationships.

Remaining silent after asking a question shows the ultimate respect for the other person. It's a gift you can give them that will be repaid to you a hundred times over with information and a deeper understanding of your patient. It's said that during a negotiation, once an offer or request is made, the person who speaks first has already lost. While this isn't always true, being silent after you've asked a question or made an important statement is a vital part of listening. The higher the quality of your questions, the more your patient will have to think in order to answer them. Don't rush them. You need to give them time to process the question and come up with the right answer so that you can help to meet their needs – needs they may not realise they have. Give them space with your silence.

By being silent, you:

- Allow your patient to reflect, think and process

- Create space for commitment (and give yourself space to think as well)
- Show respect and build further trust
- Improve your chances of success

Here's an interesting fact: 'listen' and 'silent' are made up of the same letters – something to think about before each patient interaction!

Notes on notetaking

There are two schools of thought on notetaking in patient consultations and interactions.

1. It interferes with your interaction, creates a barrier to rapport and distracts you from important non-verbal cues.
2. It's critical to capturing the patient's needs, challenges and priorities. If you're not taking notes, the patient might think you're not truly listening to and understanding them.

I recommend adopting a blend of these opposite views. Here's some guidance to consider when taking notes:

- At the start of the consultation discussion, explain to your patient that you'll take notes on important points and actions to make sure you better meet their needs.
- Only write down headlines or critical information (not everything said).

- Capture your patient's words precisely. Their language is exactly that – theirs –and your interpretation won't be as powerful to them as their own.
- While taking notes, pause to make eye contact and maintain rapport with your patient. Check what you've written as you go along by asking checking questions of your patient.
- When you're not writing, put down the pen to show you're listening. Also, you may want to put down your pen if your patient makes an important point. This dramatic pause will show you've understood the point (this can be very impactful).
- Be conscious that your notes are creating a structure you can use as a summary at the end of the meeting.

Let's look at this idea of summarising.

Summarising

Once you've asked your questions and listened to the answers, and you believe that you fully understand your patient's needs, review your notes and summarise the discussion with your patient. Summarising is important because it:

- Gives you greater relevance in the eyes of your patient
- Shows you've been listening to and that you truly understand what they need
- Creates a natural conversational flow into your discussion about treatment solutions

I suggest you use this format:
1 – Ask your patient for permission to summarise what they've told you (they will always agree).
2 – Work through your notes. Read them out loud and put a tick next to each of the needs your patient told you.
3 – Clarify each point immediately after you've read it aloud, e.g., 'Did I capture that correctly?'

After you've worked through all your notes, check to make sure nothing has been forgotten. Ask the patient, 'Have we covered everything?'

Once your patient has agreed that everything has been covered, ask for permission to move on to presenting your solutions. I suggest a joining statement such as this:

'This has been really useful, thank you for sharing this with me. I believe there are a number of ways in which I/ we can help you with the things you've explained. I'd like to share some of those with you now – would that be, OK?'

At this stage, we use closed questions because we want permission to move forward. If you've covered everything, your patient will be ready to hear what you have to say.

Before we move to the next stage there are two models for questioning mastery that will be very useful for you.

Consultative Sales Mastery: CORE MODEL & PATIENTS structure

I have two questioning models I share with my dental clients. The first is a questioning structure and flow called the CORE model and the second is the PATIENTS mnemonic that identifies all of the different areas that may be a priority consideration for your patient.

Let's cover the CORE model first. The CORE model is a structure of questions that creates a flow for your questions with your patients.

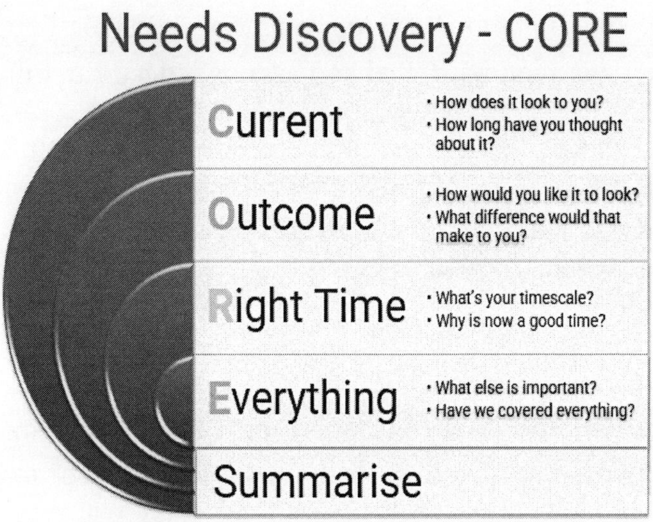

Here's the structure.

CORE stands for: Current, Outcome, Right Now, Everything. Let's look at each in turn.

Current

The initial stage is to understand what has led your patients to this position, and what's happened until now.

Ask questions like: How does your smile look to you? How long have you thought about it? How do you feel about it? Remember to listen to the patients' answers and empathise, they might find this awkward, put them at ease.

Outcome

The next stage is to help you and your patient understand what they are looking to achieve through treatment. This may be the first time they've given it this consideration and spoken it out loud, listened and acknowledged carefully.

Ask questions like: How would you like your smile to look? What difference would that make to you? How would you like to feel about it?

Right time

This stage is to understand how urgent this treatment is for the patient and how committed they are to achieving the outcome they've just described to you (and themselves).

Ask questions like: What is your timescale? How soon were you planning to start treatment? Why is now a good time for you?

Everything

The final stage is to check if the patient has had the chance to explain everything that's on their mind. This is about creating space for them to reflect, consider and convince themselves that they'd like to progress with treatment.

Ask questions like: What else is important to you? What other considerations do you have? Have we covered everything you need?

You'll notice the questions are open throughout the model and then we ask a closed question at the end to gain commitment to move forward.

Once you've completed this series of questions you should Summarise to the patient what they've told you. This summary is powerful because it clearly shows you've listened, understood and acknowledged the patient's perspective.

This structure works very well to guide the patient through their own thought process ready for them to make a decision and be prepared to move forward.

The final model we'll consider is the PATIENTS model.

This is a series of areas that the patient may be concerned about or considering as part of their decision-making process. By having them captured in this way we can ensure we cover the most important areas of the proposed treatment.

- ➢ Performance
- ➢ Aesthetics
- ➢ Time (visits)
- ➢ Investment
- ➢ Experience
- ➢ Noticeable (natural or noticeable)
- ➢ Time (longevity)
- ➢ Strength

This should be self-explanatory, but for the avoidance of doubt. Use this model to check with yourself and your patient that you are asking and explaining all of the relevant priorities for the treatment. This is a useful guide for all treatment discussions with patients.

So, we've fully understood our patient's needs, next it's time for the Solutions Discussion stage.

Take some time to review your worksheet and make a note of the HQQs you want to ask in your patient consultations. This will help you build your own tailored version of the INSPIRe Consultative Sales System.

Before we move on, reflect on this chapter and write down your thoughts in your journal or notebook.

OPTIONAL EXERCISE: QUESTIONS

Continue the optional exercise from the previous chapter.

Practise:

- Delivering your impact statement
- Asking open and probing questions
- Asking the magic question ('If you could change one thing…')
- Following the CORE Model
- Checking you've covered the relevant areas in the PATIENTS model
- Summarising your patient's needs in their language
- Confirming you've covered everything

Chapter 10: Solutions Discussion

Solutions Maxim

"People don't buy products; they buy solutions to their problems."

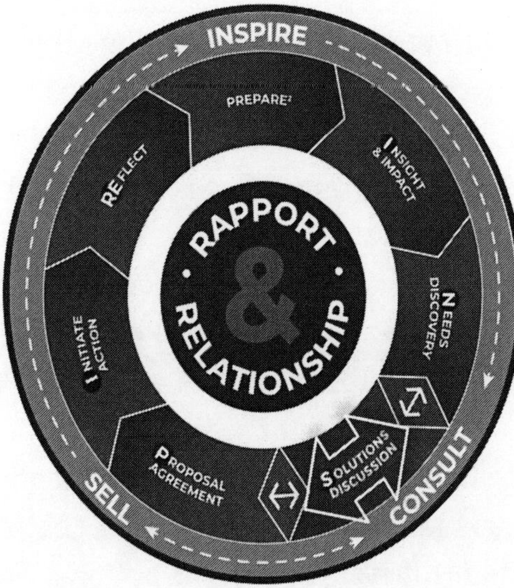

INSPIRe – Consultative Sales System: Solutions Discussion

In the second dental company I was employed by, I worked in a role that covered a portfolio of products for dental technicians and dentists. One of the portfolios was a range of denture teeth. We had a standard NHS range and a premium private range. When I joined the company, they launched a 'middle' range of teeth that were aimed at the emerging 'independent' market. The independent market was for patients who wanted a better option than the NHS but either couldn't or wouldn't stretch their budget to private treatment options. In the first few months of launch the product was well received but demand for it was lower than anticipated. The team needed a new approach.

In response, our marketing team developed a product called the 'Denture Selector'. The Denture Selector was a Perspex display case that presented all three sets of upper and lower anterior teeth from our range. Each product in the range was accompanied by a patient persona, with a lifestyle story. There were features that accompanied each of the sets of teeth, these features and the associated benefits improved with each increase in the range. As a team we were able to present the Denture Selector as a patient education (and sales) tool that helped our dentist and dental technician customers explain the differences between NHS, Independent and Private treatment options. The impact of this tool was incredible, we could just about keep up with demand for Denture Selectors.

The aim of the Denture Selector was to launch an independent range of teeth, but it did so much more than that for the business. Our customers were able to use the Denture Selector to tell a story to their patients. Explain what the differences were between each of the treatment options and help the patient understand why they would choose independent and private treatments. Demand for all three teeth in the range increased, which we hadn't expected. Just as surprising was the feedback from our dentists about how the Denture Selector helped them in patient discussions.

Their ability to explain the differences went beyond denture patients, which seemed to help patients understand the differences in the service offered by the practice. It supported the discussions with patients to upgrade private treatment and payment plans. The more patients chose private plans, the more success stories the dentist had to share with other patients. Over time, confidence increased, and momentum was built that became unstoppable.

Things have moved on significantly since then, with the evolution of digital dentistry it's now possible to demonstrate to a patient in 'real time' how their smile and oral function can be improved. Yet many dentists haven't made the leap, or if they have, they're not taking full advantage of the opportunity that's at their fingertips! I remind you to recognise the potential for your practice and your business. They say, "a picture paints a thousand words", it's true. Remember also that stories can be powerful motivators for patient behaviour too.

Combining both of these principles with our Solutions Discussion stage will transform your ability to present treatment options and create a truly compelling patient experience.

Why stories matter

So why have I told you this story? At the Solutions Discussion stage of the INSPIRe Consultative Sales System, the focus is on positioning your solution to meet your patient's needs. This positioning is crucial and will set you apart. Bill Gates once said that 'if you show people the problems and you show people the solutions, they will be moved to act'.[14] This perfectly sums up the next stage of our process. If you connect problems (or needs) with the solutions you can offer, your clients will feel compelled to act. If you can do so with a compelling story or anecdote, you'll captivate your patients in a way that your competition won't be able to match if they're selling using facts and figures. Stories are always more powerful than statistics.

I hope that as you read the story you started to think about how you could more creatively position your own treatment options. This is a great time to capture those thoughts. You may also want to write down these questions in your journal or notebook and answer them as you work through the chapter:

- What is your story (about you, the practice, your treatments & patient experience)?
- How could you display your uniqueness?
- What is the most interesting and compelling insight you could share?
- How could you weave your knowledge and experience into a fascinating anecdote?
- What would captivate your patients?
- How could you give your patients a true experience with your product or service?

14 'Net fuels Live 8 extravaganza' (BBC News, 2005), http://news.bbc. co.uk/1/hi/technology/4648003.stm, accessed 28 September 2020

- Which specialist treatment options should you focus more on?
- What patient case studies and examples should you be referring to on a regular basis with your patients?
- How can you better harness the great work you've done with other patients?

"With the advent of digital dentistry comes the ability to harness images, pictures and patient success stories. If you're a digital practice, start to build your library of patient 'before' and 'after' images.

As you build a variety of treatments and patient demographics you'll find it becomes easier to convince patients that you're the optimal choice for providing those treatment options."

Discuss, don't pitch

At this stage, there's a reason why we use the word 'discussion' and not 'pitch'. During your presentation of treatment options, it's important to keep checking in with your patient. Many people get this stage wrong and think that they should have been "pitching" from the start. Actually, they shouldn't be pitching at all – it should always be a discussion. This is why people become so resistant to selling, because they've experienced too many poor pitches. Notice, we're at the fourth stage of our process before we even consider discussing what we can provide, which is intentional.

Reminder: if you don't fully understand your patient's needs at this stage, you aren't relevant, and your chances of success will plummet.

Instead of pitching, have a solutions discussion to make sure the patient is following what you're saying and that they believe you. If you don't, you risk losing your patient along the way. When you choose to have a discussion (rather than to pitch), the conversation flows, even though at this stage you'll likely be doing a lot of the talking. A discussion format allows your patient to give you feedback, which you can address immediately. The patient won't have to wait until you've finished talking to address something that's bothering them. It's a more effective way to alleviate your patient's concerns, and you and your patient will naturally end up with the right solution to meet your joint needs.

Positioning your treatment options – features, advantages and benefits

Being clear on the features of your patient treatment options is fundamental to a successful solution discussion. Without this knowledge, you won't be consistent or influential in your patient consultations.

When you're positioning the treatment option (as part of the discussion), it's important to understand the difference between features, advantages and benefits. The differences are subtle but important:

- Feature – what the treatment/ product does or has

- Advantage – how it's better than other treatments or features
- Benefit – the [unique] value your patient will get from that treatment feature.

Some people will naturally consider the advantages or benefits of something (once they understand the features), but not everyone thinks this way. When you're explaining a solution that incorporates technology that is service based or that is complex in any way, always set out the features, advantages and benefits to your patient. No exceptions. If you leave it to your patient to figure out, you'll risk the impact being diluted, at best, or completely lost. As you explain the features, advantages and benefits, in this order, be enthusiastic to engage and excite your patient about the way in which your solution will help them. And of course, you can weave in a story or a patient testimonial. Here's a simple structure to help you remember how to position the features, advantages and benefits consistently:

1. The [insert treatment option] offers you [insert feature].
2. It's better than [insert other option] because [insert advantage].
3. Which means that [insert benefit].

Once you find a flow you can shorten the structure.

Here are a few examples using clear aligners:

> The [Clear Aligner System] offers you [an invisible and incredibly strong material].

> Many patients say it's better than [brackets & wires] because [it looks natural, and they rarely break].
>
> Which means that [you're less likely to need emergency appointments for repairs].
>
> AND
>
> They are [removable].
>
> Unlike [brackets & wires] so [mealtimes are easier].
>
> Which means that [you can still eat and drink normally].
>
> AND
>
> They are [clear trays with smooth edges].
>
> Unlike [brackets & wires] so [there are no sharp wires or bracket edges].
>
> Which means [you don't experience any scratches or sores].
>
> AND
>
> They need [less adjustment appointments].
>
> Unlike [brackets & wires] so [there are fewer visits and appointments].
>
> Which means [you reduce your travelling time and appointment time].

You don't have to use this exact format, but it's a structure to start from. As you can see from this example, your solution is likely to have multiple features, advantages and benefits, so you can use this structure to lay them out and make sure you cover them comprehensively with your patient.

The most powerful piece of this structure is the benefit to your patient – you must ensure the benefit is clear and compelling. So how do you know that you've explained your solution's benefits? There's a way to sense-check this.

The 'so what?' rule

The 'so what?' The rule is a tried and tested way to confirm that the benefit you're explaining to your patient is just that: a true benefit. The rule is simple: the benefit to your patient is only a benefit if the question 'so what?' doesn't undermine it.

When you're writing or planning benefits, test each one with 'so what?' to make sure you're stating a benefit and not a feature or advantage. As a rule of thumb, a true benefit will generate a better outcome for the patient or improve their treatment experience.

The outcome or experience can be linked to the patient's needs that they've explained to you through your Needs Discovery stage earlier. Please bear this rule in mind during your solutions discussions, you'll always be relevant to your patient.

The solution loop

To show the patient that you understand them, loop back to their needs when explaining the features, advantages and benefits of the treatment option. In doing so, you'll create a bespoke solution for your patient. It's as simple as adding a line which simply states the patient's relevant need. If we added a solution loop to our earlier first example, we'd end up with this:

- The [Clear Aligner System] offers you [an invisible and incredibly strong material].
- Many patients say it's better than [brackets & wires] because [it looks natural, and they rarely break].
- Which means that [you're less likely to need emergency appointments for repairs].
- You mentioned earlier that you wanted the treatment to be discreet and that you wanted the treatment to take up as little of your time as possible. This treatment option will help you achieve both of those goals.

While this is displayed as a series of statements, remember that your patient consultation should be a discussion. Allow the conversation to flow and pay attention to your patient's responses. If they're showing positive body language (nodding, smiling or giving you an encouraging look), let them process what you've said.

Link each of the features, advantages and benefits to the needs the patient expressed in the Needs Discovery stage of the process. You can check them against the notes from your earlier summary. This is critical to gain the patient's acceptance of the treatment solution. Then clarify that they agree that the solution you're discussing meets their needs. You can use a closed or open question to do this. For example:

- Do you agree that this will give you what you need?
- Does this sound like it will work for you?

At this stage, you'll likely have gained acceptance. The patient should be able to clearly see that your solution will meet their needs. If there are any concerns that haven't yet been raised, this is the point to clarify and deal with them.

I've developed a worksheet I use with clients and teams. It's called the FABSOL worksheet, and it will help you position your solution's features, advantages, benefits and incorporate a solution loop. There's a blank template based on the Clear Aligner example from this chapter.

You can download a copy of the FABSOL template here: https://bit.ly/FABSOL-ICS.

A note about unique selling points

I'm sure you've come across the term 'USP' or 'unique selling point' before. I prefer the term 'unique selling benefit'. As we've discussed, it's important to position your solution's benefits appropriately, otherwise the patient will think or ask, 'so what?'. If your treatment option (or treatment with you) has a unique feature, understanding how it will benefit your patient is arguably more important than the feature itself!

If your solution does have a unique selling benefit, you'll have a strong advantage over your competition. And now you know how to position that uniqueness in the right way so that your patient will appreciate it and you'll be relevant to them. You should consider how to create a USP from yourself, your team and your practice. An effective way to do this is with a personal commitment. Stating to your patient that you will do "everything possible to ensure they get the best outcome and experience possible" can provide powerful reassurance. This creates differentiation from other providers who lead with anything other than quality.

Consultative Sales Mastery: The Power of language

Language is important in your patient consultations, mostly language is unconscious, we don't think about the words we use. There are certain words and phrases that can be beneficial in conversations and others that can create resistance. We may not be aware of them. Here are a few examples that will help you become more intentional with your language.

Investment, not Cost or Price

A principle that can be impactful on your patient consultations is the removal or the words 'cost' or 'price'. Instead use the word 'investment'. We want our patients to think of treatment with us as an investment in their oral health and their smile.

As people we form strong associations through language. When we hear the word cost or price, we associate it with losing something. When we hear the word investment, we associate it with gaining something. This subtle language change can help patients to associate gaining value from our treatment. If they are speaking with other potential providers who talk about features and costs, and we discuss benefits and investment, we will be seen differently.

'Towards' and 'Away'

In decision making, we all have motivations that are 'towards' what we want and 'away' from what we don't want. For many people one of these perspectives will be more influential in their thinking than the other. In our patient consultations we can listen for clues. If a patient says "I don't like the way my teeth look" or ". As you ask more questions, they continue to focus on how much they dislike their smile, they are likely to have a preference for the language. Positioning accordingly will make them feel more influential.

On the other hand, you will have patients who say "I want a nicer smile" or "I'd like whiter teeth" they are more likely to have a preference for 'towards' language. Noticing the differences and using the patient's preferred language will help you be more relevant and meet your patient's treatment needs.

There will be patients who use a combination of both 'directions', and in when discussing with them you should use both too.

Making time for non-clinical professional development

The longer you work with your patients, the greater their expectations of you will become. That's a good thing. They'll come to see you as a trusted source of information about dentistry as a specialism and the profession you're working in. I encourage you to embrace this expectation and be proactive in your development within your field of expertise. Here are some suggestions:

- Be intentional about developing your specialist areas of expertise
- Read industry/professional publications
- Know the trends and major initiatives in the marketplace
- Identify the opinion leaders and what they're saying (quotes are valuable)
- Understand what's controversial and why
- Know the useful statistics – popular treatment options, growth rates, key challenges, etc.

- Learn about the latest techniques and principles
- Know your competition – what they're saying, current products, key issues they're facing, etc.
- Know the specific unique advantages you and your team have

If you dedicate a set amount of time in your diary to learn about the market (I suggest thirty minutes a week), within a couple of months, you'll have developed a level of expertise that will astound you. You'll then be more confident in-patient consultations and build credibility in your practice and the wider dental market in which you work. I'm sure you already know that professional development will take you far over time.

Reflecting on your questioning

Once you have completed this Solutions Discussion work, you'll likely identify more questions that you need to ask your patients to better understand their needs as they relate to your solution. This is a good time to consider the bigger picture. Getting clear on your solution's features, advantages and benefits will have helped you position your solution and link back to your patient's needs. Now, it's time to update your HQQs from the last chapter. This isn't about assuming your patient's needs but helping you prepare to meet them more effectively.

I recommend referring to your HQQs bank and updating it – add or amend questions as necessary after reviewing this chapter. I also suggest reviewing your FABSOL Working

Table and noting which features, advantages and benefits you should address in your patient consultations. These must link to known or unrealised patient needs as part of the solutions loop. Finally, review the INSPIRe worksheet, so that you are building a consistent and comprehensive approach.

You've had a meaningful solutions discussion with your patient. You've addressed their needs, clearly laid out the benefits they'll receive from your solution, engaged them with your storytelling and demonstrated your credibility with your expertise, evidence and patient referrals. It's time to make a proposal.

Before we move on, reflect on this chapter and write down your thoughts in your journal or notebook.

OPTIONAL EXERCISE: FEATURES, ADVANTAGES AND BENEFITS

Write down a series of features, advantages and benefits your solution offers (using the structure presented in this chapter). Capture how these can be part of a solution loop (back to your patient's needs).

Then continue the optional exercise from the previous chapter.

Practise:

- Summarising your patients' needs in their language
- Delivering the features, advantages and benefits of your product/service
- Linking these to your patient's needs using the solution loop
- Checking that your patient is ready for you to make a proposal

Chapter 11: Proposal Agreement

Propose Maxim

'You only find out if your patient wants to proceed, when you ask'

INSPIRe – Consultative Sales System: Proposal Agreement

Early in my sales career I was apprehensive of asking my customers for commitment or to place an order. I hated it; I would avoid it almost all of the time. I'd find myself in a customer discussion about a new product and they seemed interested. I'd explain about the product, the customer would be nodding and showing positive body language. I'd talk a bit longer and then pause, there would be an awkward silence and I'd say something like "Would you like to think about it?". More often than not, the customer would then say "Yes, leave it with me and I'll think about it".

I'd then leave, make a note in my notebook and my diary for the next time I'd see them. The next time I followed up the next time, they'd completely forgotten about our previous discussion, or ordered more of their current product so they no longer had a need for the product we'd previously discussed. Even after I'd been trained in sales I struggled to ask for commitment, until I worked with my sales manager, Sally, who helped me 'reframe' my perspective.

Sally and I were calling on customers together and after one call she asked me what was holding me back from asking for the order. At that point I'd been telling myself I was doing all I could and that customers would buy when they were ready. What I hadn't figured out was that customers are ready to buy in that moment. When given the option to 'think about it' their enthusiasm wins, and life takes over. They don't think about it again. She asked me a series of questions that changed my perspective.

I'm paraphrasing, but the questions were similar to these.

"How confident are you that the solution you're offering will really benefit your customer?

Once you've got your customers excited, do you think it's fair that you leave it open-ended?

How can the customer believe in the solution if you aren't confident enough to ask them for commitment?

How could you manage your own discomfort, so you can ask your customer for the order?

What if every customer is expecting you to ask for commitment and is disappointed when you don't?

What question could you ask that feels natural to you and makes the customer feel confident to place an order at that moment?"

These questions opened my eyes, I found an answer for each of them and in a short time, I was able to ask every customer for commitment. The question I came to like best was "Is that something you'd like me to do for you?" My world was transformed!

I share this story with you because at this stage of the process it can feel like it's the most difficult, but it should feel like the easiest. Let's learn how.

Checking in with the patient

Once you've reached Proposal Agreement in the sales system, you're coming to the closing stage. If you've followed the INSPIRe Consultative Sales System correctly, you and your patient will be looking to confirm the details and move forward. This is the point at which you should make a proposal and gain commitment. I use the term 'proposal agreement' as it signals to you that this is the time to make a proposal and that the aim is to gain the patient's agreement to that proposal. Agreement builds the foundation for a strong, positive, and long-term relationship with your patient.

Before making your proposal, check in with the patient by asking a simple question. For example:

- Is there anything else we need to cover before we discuss the proposal for treatment?
- Are you happy for me to make a proposal?
- If I make a proposal, do you have everything you need to make a decision?

These types of questions will enable your patient to either agree to move forward, seek clarification on items they're uncertain about or raise an objection. Once they confirm their agreement, you'll move to the next stage of the system (which we'll look at next). If they're seeking clarification, address any questions or reservations. If they raise an objection, you must work through the relevant steps to resolve it.

Handling objections

Nobody is perfect! There will likely be times when you find yourself close to the end of the treatment discussion, close to gaining a commitment, and suddenly your patient throws in an objection, taking the wind out of your sails. Sound familiar?

The best way to approach objections is to remind yourself of the INSPIRe Consultative Sales System. Return to the Needs

Discovery stage. Remember, the process moves in both directions between Proposal Agreement, Solutions Discussion and Needs Discovery. An objection means your patient has an unmet need. It's useful to consider that an objection is a signal that the patient is seriously considering your proposal. See it as a positive sign.

Selling sometimes involves dealing with egos. You might have a patient who's downright awkward and will make statements that seem contrary just for the sake of it. We've all met these people. Before a patient consultation, one of the best things you can do is to consciously park your ego at the surgery door. I recommend picturing yourself doing this. It can be a calming part of your personal preparation. It's easy to get drawn into disagreements with difficult patients, and before you know it, you'll find yourself in a tit-for-tat debate that you cannot win (if you win the argument, you lose the patient!).

If you're faced with a patient who is clearly in the wrong but won't be told otherwise – perhaps they're making incorrect statements about the marketplace or treatment options – there's a simple and effective way to handle the situation:

- Don't agree or disagree with them (agreeing can reinforce their point while disagreeing can cause an argument).
- Acknowledge and understand their perspective.
- Stay neutral on the topic; remain objective.
- Take responsibility for the misunderstanding, that way you can proactively manage it.

- Allow your patients to vent (often that's all they want) and ask only light questions.
- Link back to their needs and return to the INSPIRe Consultative Sales System.

This simple, effective approach will help you enormously with difficult patients.

Objections will vary, but generally they fall into one of three categories:

- Misunderstanding
- Scepticism
- Genuine needs objection

Let's walk through them and look at the ways you can handle each one.

Misunderstanding

A misunderstanding happens when your patient doesn't fully understand the way in which your treatment option works. It's fairly common for people to raise objections based on a misunderstanding. The best way to handle a misunderstanding is to take these steps:

- Empathise, and then clarify the misunderstanding: 'What exactly is the concern?'
- Listen to, understand and summarise the objection.
- Apologise for the fact that you weren't clear the first time around.

- Explain that you may have caused a misunderstanding and clarify that treatment options will deliver what your patient needs.

Confirming that the misunderstanding has been addressed. This is the most straightforward objection to resolve. Once your patient confirms it has been addressed, you can move forward.

Scepticism

Scepticism is when your patient doesn't believe that your treatment option will do what you're saying it will do. To put it another way, 'It's too good to be true!' When someone displays scepticism, it's easy to become dismissive and defend your position forcefully. This will only make your patient more sceptical. The best way to address scepticism is to be prepared for it. This is where evidence, demonstrations and testimonials from other patients about how well your solution works are highly valuable. The following steps will help you to address scepticism:

- Empathise, and then clarify the scepticism: 'What exactly is the concern?'
- Listen to, understand and summarise the objection.
- Ask what evidence the patient would like to see to give them confidence that your solution will deliver what they need.

If your patient isn't able to tell you what would convince them, consider: A practical demonstration/ example

- Showing patient testimonials & videos
- Presenting evidence and case studies
- Sharing a similar patient story

Scepticism can slow down the decision making but must be addressed fully or your patient could become a wider issue for your business; if you can't convince them, they may become vocal about it to other potential patients. Take the time needed to convince them. Be patient and find out what it will take to prove to your patient that your treatment solution will do what you say it will do. Scepticism presents you with an opportunity – your patient could become a significant advocate once you've convinced them. Imagine your patient saying, 'Well I didn't believe it at first, but the treatment solution did everything I was told it would!' Successfully address their scepticism, and this is a probable outcome.

You also have an opportunity to negotiate here. Make your patient a proposition. For example: 'So if I prove to you that our treatment solution delivers the result you want, will you agree to write/ record a testimonial?' This might be a fair trade – a guaranteed result for an evaluation of your service. And delivered in the right way, this type of negotiation can further strengthen your patient relationship.

Genuine needs objection

This is the trickiest objection of them all. A patient will make genuine needs objections when your treatment solution meets some but not all of their needs. The best way to handle this situation is to take these steps:

- Empathise, and then clarify the genuine needs objection: 'What exactly is the concern?'
- Listen to, understand and summarise the objection.
- Be honest about the mismatch between your patient's needs and your treatment solution.
- Highlight the needs your patient has that your solution does meet.
- Ask your patient to prioritise their needs: 'Which is most important?'
- Consider what you could do to minimise the treatment solution's shortfall.
- Ask your patient, 'What would need to happen for you to be happy with this treatment solution?'

If your patient decides that your solution isn't right for them after you've taken these steps, you may have to accept it. The final thing you can do is ask your patient to sleep on it and agree on a time to have a follow-up discussion. As you wrap up the consultation, remind the patient of the needs your solution does meet and let them know you genuinely hope you can help them. Before your follow-up discussion, speak with other members of your team who may have had the same objection and overcome it (ask around the practice).

You can then send a message to your patient with the additional information or wait until your follow-up discussion to give them the new facts you've discovered. This may help your patient decide. If not, remember, you can't please everyone.

The more objections you handle, the better you'll get at it. And objections can really help with patient loyalty. If you have to work hard to convince the patient, they may be someone who is very hard to please, more difficult for other dentists to treat and become more loyal to you because you made the effort to go the extra mile to satisfy them.

The proposal

Making your proposal should be a straightforward step at this point. Be confident, clear and concise. You've worked hard to get here and have earned the right to make a positive proposal that meets your patient's needs. Make sure your language is concise and confident. Don't pose your proposal as a question – it's a statement and it's tailored to your patient, so be proud to make it.

Consultative Sales Mastery: Negotiations

Using a framework

When you're making a proposal, it's easy to feel as though the hard work is done. You may want to just get it over with and move on. But remember, this is an important moment for your patient. They're making an investment in you, so don't rush the process. Focus on making the experience positive for your patient, from start to finish.

For some patients, negotiation is a part of the proposal process – they will always believe they can get a better deal. Your job is to help them realise that your proposal is the best investment possible.

It's important to take these two key factors into account when discounting your price:

- Any discount given to your patient will negatively impact your practice revenue
- Discounting will impact practice profitability, and there may be a need to adjust performance related bonuses (if in place).

If you're able to offer discounts on price or show flexibility on aspects of your solution and understand the impact these things will have on your business, you have some negotiating leverage.

Through negotiating courses I've taken over the years, I've learned several useful principles and techniques. I have 6 Tips I share for negotiating that clients find very useful. Here they are:

1 – *Take your time, get comfortable*

Very often when people negotiate with us, we can feel incredibly uncomfortable, that's human nature kicking in. We don't like being asked for something we don't want to give, and we don't like awkward moments. In a negotiation, the person that stays calm, present and slows down the pace is the person that generally comes off best. Learn to see negotiations as small windows in time where you can stay calm and relaxed. Just taking this perspective on them will help you manage them much better.

2 – *Show a reaction, switch the pressure*

There is a principle in negotiating called 'The Professional Flinch'. Professional negotiators use it to great effect. They pretend that the offer being made has caused them pain – as if someone has physically hurt them. They recoil, scrunch up their faces and squint as they draw air through their teeth. Think about watching a video of someone slipping on ice and landing hard. You'll likely flinch. This is the reaction they're recreating.

After they flinch, they wait in silence. The switch in pressure has been made, the other person now feels intense pressure, and the balance of power has shifted. I'm not suggesting you go to this extreme, but I am suggesting you show a reaction. Very often when people make requests from us for unreasonable discounts or reductions, we don't respond at all out of awkwardness. That's signalling to the other person that they are in a strong position and when we react, they realise they're not and maybe they should reconsider their request.

You can use a version of the professional flinch whenever you feel that unreasonable demands are being made on you or that someone is behaving in a way that you don't think is right. Watch how powerful it is.

3 – Focus on the Outcome

In a negotiation we can sometimes get carried away by the emotion of the discussion and that can make us blinkered to the outcome. When negotiating with patients, stay focused on the treatment outcome, wanting to treat the patient in the best way possible and forming a long-term loyal relationship between you and them. It's not personal, keep things light-hearted and you both enjoy the discussion and are more likely to find agreement.

4 - List the 'points of negotiation'

I recommend a structured pricing policy to ensure everyone in the practice understands the pricing structure. If you are going to offer promotional deals or pricing discounts you will need to consider in advance what they are and how long they're available. The other considerations are the conditions you need patients to meet in exchange for the promotion or discount. Here are some examples of the This list isn't exhaustive, but it should give you some ideas:

- Payment in full and upfront
- A written or video recommendation following successful treatment
- A case-study document or video
- A referral or introduction to another patient
- Signing up to a comprehensive follow-up treatment plan
- A Positive Social Media post/ series (depending on the influence of the patient)

Having this structure in place means you will be better prepared for each discussion and when you're prepared, you're more confident.

5 – 'Trade' don't 'Give'

In business it's fundamental not to give something away without asking for something in return. You should be clear on what you want in return for making a discount or promotion (as discussed at the start of this section). The recommended phrase in this situation is 'If you… then I…' This makes any discount you give conditional on the exchange with the patient. Get comfortable using this phrase. It will enable you to negotiate more effectively.

Here's an example. Imagine your patient is asking for a 10% discount on the treatment proposal and you're able to meet this request but would like them to commit to becoming a patient of the practice on a Denplan membership scheme. You might say something like this:

'Well, the proposal I've made gives you access to our best pricing. However, if you are prepared to become a patient of the practice and sign up to our Denplan membership then I would be able to give you a 10% discount on the treatment.'

This gives you greater control of the negotiation. Silence comes into play again here as well (see Chapter 9 for a recap on silence). After you've made your negotiating statement, be silent and wait for your patient's response. In a negotiation, the first person to speak following a proposal is more likely to accept the other person's proposal. Throughout a negotiation there may be several statements made and positions taken. This is good as it shows progress. Make sure you continue to use the phrase 'If you, then I…'.

6 - *Price anchoring*

When discussing pricing with your patient in a negotiation, it's important to 'anchor' your price. This simply means stating your price over and over. By doing this, you start to condition your patient to your price and not the price they've requested or stated. Even if you offer a discount, refer to your starting price. At an unconscious level this gives you greater authority in the negotiation.

Just as your proposal should be stated clearly and assertively, so should your price. It's a statement, not a question – be confident and direct. This sets you up to anchor your price during any negotiation. If your patient raises a challenge, you can say or ask something along these lines:

- £3,750 [whatever the price is] provides excellent value for the quality and service we discussed.
- How close to £3,750 can you get?
- So, in principle, you could commit to the price of £3,750 if I could give you a X% discount.

There are many ways in which you can anchor your price. The key is to remember to do so – don't be drawn into referencing your patient's price request. Keeping the discussion focused on your price keeps the balance of power in your favour.

Many dental professionals simply 'give away' a discount or service without asking for anything in return. From this point on, make a commitment to knowing what you want and making the request of your patient in exchange for meeting their demands.

In your journal or notebook, write down a list of ideas for negotiation requests you could make of your patients. With this list you'll be forearmed. As we learned in Chapter 4, preparation gives you greater confidence, control and power in your patient consultations.

There are many resources available for negotiation. If you want to become more proficient, I suggest doing further research. One particularly good book is Never Split the Difference, by Chris Voss and Tahl Raz. It's an original look at negotiations, seen through the lens of hostage negotiations. It's a compelling read littered with stories and anecdotes that offer practical principles for effective negotiations.

Take some time to review your worksheet and make note of the key components that should be included in your proposals as part of your patient meetings. These can be headlines, criteria or negotiating points. This will further strengthen your personalised INSPIRe Consultative Sales System.

Before we move on, reflect on this chapter and write down your thoughts in your journal or notebook.

15 C Voss and T Raz, Never Split the Difference: Negotiating as if your life depended on it (Random House, 2017)

OPTIONAL EXERCISE: THE PROPOSAL

Continue the optional exercise from the previous chapter.

Practise:

- Ensuring that your patient is ready for you to make a proposal
- Delivering a confident, concise and compelling proposal
- Handling the objections your patient raises using the structure in this chapter
- Clarifying that your patient is satisfied that their objections have been addressed

Chapter 12: Initiate Action

Initiate Maxim

'Clear, time-bound actions inspire commitment & momentum'

INSPIRe – Consultative Sales System: Initiate Action

When I first started my coaching business in 2018, I started conversations with some of my previous colleagues, managers, peers and friends. I wanted to let them know I'd started a business, understand more about their work and share my plans. Ultimately, I was seeking to understand if there was a fit between what they needed and the coaching services I was providing. I used the INSPIRe process as my guide for those conversations.

I recall a potential client who was incredibly keen to embark on a significant programme. The plan was to train and coach their leadership team to become more emotionally intelligent leaders. My potential client was the Managing Director of a significant dental & medical company and the decision maker for the programme. He'd experienced many challenges managing his board of directors and wanted to work on a series of sessions to accompany the work he was doing with his team.

We have agreed to the framework for the programme and had numerous discussions about structure, sessions, individuals and timing. I had been creating clear actions and scheduling follow up discussions, to the point where I believe the programme was confirmed. For some reason in the penultimate meeting, I left the next steps with my client to complete. I then became busy with other client work and forgot to follow up with my client. By the time I did, he'd reflected on the programme and felt he needed more time to consider if it was the 'optimal approach' (his words).

When I followed up with him 3 months later, he still had not acted. His issues were still present, but he'd become resigned to them and wasn't sure they were addressable. It's fascinating what happens when we're given time to rationalise our situation. Inertia is a powerful force that can only be overturned by the initiation of action.

As an experienced business leader, trainer and coach, I recognise myself that if I don't follow this structure, I notice clients are disengaged. In particular, as in this situation, I found I could put in a significant amount of effort to learn about the client, summarise their needs and gain agreement that my solution was what they needed. If I wasn't able to "initiate action" as a result of the conversation the opportunity dissipated.

Your patient conversations are the same, and when people are ready to commit and purchase, we must ensure we meet that readiness by initiating action. If we don't the patient's desire can waiver, they may rationalise that they can 'live with' their situation and inertia set in. Initiate Action is a critical phase in the consultative sales process.

Gaining commitment

You could be forgiven for thinking that at this stage of the consultation, the agreement is made, you can pat yourself on the back and move on to the next patient. But it's vital to make and gain a commitment. This is what the Initiate Action phase is all about. It's the obligation that ensures what you've discussed with your patient happens. Without this final stage, you'll find that 'stuff' gets in the way of your patient moving forward with what you've agreed in your consultation.

Once your patient leaves your practice, their life goes on, the emails flood in, the office door gets knocked on, their partner calls, they have a crisis to deal with, or a fire to put out – any number of things will throw them off course. It's not personal. In today's busy world, if you don't get your patients to commit to Initiate action, there's a high risk that what you've agreed on won't happen. Getting things right at this stage will give your results and patient case acceptance a significant boost.

You may feel like you're overdoing it at this point, perhaps creating a 'hard sell' situation. But you're not. Having come this far with your patient – you've identified that they have a real need, you have a solution, and you and the patient agree that the proposal is mutually beneficial – you owe it to them to complete the consultative sale successfully. That means making sure that you both follow through on the actions required to complete the transaction or finalise commitment to the proposal. It's an appropriate time to be absolutely clear that you're confirming the proposal and the corresponding actions. I suggest asking a simple assumptive question in a conversational style. Something similar to the following:

- So, are you happy if we go ahead with the treatment proposal?
- Is there anything else we need to consider before we go ahead and confirm the treatment proposal?
- If we were to confirm today, would there be anything else you need?

This final check allows your patient to agree and allows you to progress. Be silent and listen. If the patient has any reservations, remember INSPIRe and work back through their needs, your solution and any objections. If necessary, adjust your proposal. It's as simple as that.

Once you have an agreement, summarise what has been agreed and confirm the actions that must be taken to finalise the transaction and ensure the deal goes ahead.

At this stage, you and the patient should agree to:

- The actions your team will take to start the treatment plan (and the timing of those actions/ appointments)
- The actions your patient will take (and the timing of those actions)
- Next steps (documentation to be signed, financial plans to be arranged, appointments to be booked)
- Who else will need to be involved and who will follow up with them, and when?
- A date and time for a follow-up discussion if required (to make sure everything is to your patient's satisfaction)
- Appointment date (to start treatment)

A simple plan that outlines who will do what by when produces clarity and ensures commitment. If you haven't been completing this final stage in your patient interactions and start doing so now, you'll l notice that the rate at which your patients go from simply saying they'll do something (and then your team have to chase them) to doing what you've both agreed, will increase dramatically.

Clear, time-bound actions inspire commitment & momentum.

Consultative Sales Mastery: The Power of Feedback and Gratitude

Feedback

Surprisingly, few dental professionals ask for feedback at the end of a patient consultation. Most want to finish quickly and move on to the next appointment. But if you make a point of asking for feedback at the end of every patient consultation, you'll learn what really works for your patient and what you need to do to make yourself and your practice even better in the future.

You might not get feedback every time – if your patients aren't used to being asked for feedback, they may not be able to think of anything. But if your patient cannot think of any concrete feedback, they're likely to say that they're satisfied with the treatment, or the outcome of it. This in itself is a powerful positive reinforcement for you and your patient. They have confirmed for themselves, out loud (which further reinforces their point of view), that you've met their needs and their expectations.

When asking for feedback, do so with two simple questions:

> Before we finish today, I wonder if I could ask for your feedback on the treatment. How did you find it?

Listen, be silent and take the feedback on board (make a note). Follow up with:

> What would you change?

Once again listen, be silent and take the feedback on board (make a note).

As always, thank you for your patience with their feedback. You may also need to respond to feedback directly if the patient does recommend changes. This feedback has the power to continually elevate the patient experience you provide.

The final thank you

After every patient meeting, take the time to genuinely appreciate your patient. They have the freedom to spend their time however they wish and choose any of the dental practices in the marketplace. They have chosen you! Think about it for a moment – this is a significant compliment. Recognise it and declare it to your patient. Expressing your sincere thanks and appreciation for their time, and their trust in you to satisfy their needs, is the perfect way to show your patient how much you value them. It will make them feel justified in their choice, it will reinforce your relationship and it will significantly strengthen the loyalty your patient shows you.

If you can generate a positive emotion in your patient when you end an appointment with them, this will be their lasting memory of you and your practice. Appreciation is incredibly powerful. Sincere gratitude can create real warmth in a relationship, so grant this to your patient at the end of every consultation. Then, every time your patient cleans their teeth or appreciates their smile they'll think of you, and every time they think of you, they'll think about how well you listen, how you genuinely meet their needs and how you're grateful that they're a patient at your practice. This creates a positive cycle in your patient's mind and emotional centre that will cement your relationship with them beyond the consultation or even the practice. You win their heart!

Take some time to review your worksheet and make note of how to incorporate Initiate action into your patient consultations to strengthen your personalised INSPIRe Consultative Sales System.

Before we move on, reflect on this chapter and write down your thoughts in your journal or notebook.

OPTIONAL EXERCISE: TAKING ACTION

Continue the optional exercise from the previous chapter.

Practise:

- Finalising the list of actions, you and your patient will take
- Agreeing on the next appointment/ consultation
- Asking for feedback
- Expressing your thanks and appreciation

Chapter 13: Reflection (Self-coaching)

Reflection Maxim

'We reach our highest potential though continuous improvement.'

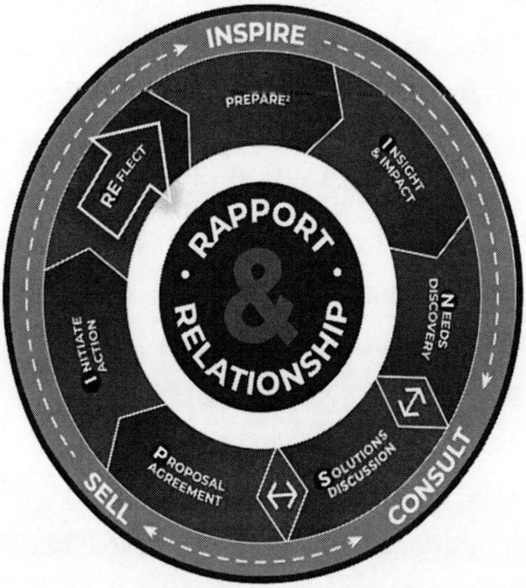

INSPIRe – Consultative Sales System: Reflection

When I was working as a sales representative in 2002, I covered a lot of miles in my car. I'd while away the time listening to the radio and calling my colleagues. One weekend, I visited my mother-in-law, Pam, with my wife and children. Pam had just completed an MSc in Health Management and was working as a manager in the NHS. She had a good career and had been interested in her professional development for some years. I talked to her about my career aspirations, and Pam told me that she had a couple of books I might be interested in reading – they had helped in her development: Unlimited Power, by Anthony Robbins,[16] and Learned Optimism, by Martin Seligman.[17]

She also asked me if I'd seen Tony Robbins in action. At that stage, I hadn't. She loaded a video on her computer then said, 'I've seen it before. I'll leave you to it.' I watched in awe. Tony Robbins' ability to connect with people and help them transform their lives seemed effortless. That was a significant day in my life. I am committed to my personal and professional development. I started buying (and, this is crucial, reading and listening to) books and audio programmes about self-development, business, high performance and personal success. I realised that to generate the level of success I wanted in my life, I simply had to learn the necessary skills. I also realised that I had a significant amount of time at my disposal – time that I was currently spend time listening to the radio and making non-essential phone calls. I worked out what I wanted for my career and then went about reading the books and listening to programmes by the best in the field. Once I gained the knowledge, I implemented what I learned. I got so much better at my job, I enjoyed it more and my career took off.

I took the approach of improving myself to improve my career. During my time as a dental salesperson, key account manager, sales manager, business leader and business

16 A Robbins, Unlimited Power: The new science of personal achievement (Pocket Books, 2001). 17 M Seligman, Learned Optimism: How to change your mind and your life (Free Press, 2002)

owner focused on the incremental improvements I could make each day.

It's incredible how much you can improve over the course of a year, broken down into months and weeks. Self-development and personal growth give you confidence, and it helps you realise that you can achieve any goal you set for yourself over time. There are so many examples of people who have harnessed the power of reflection to stimulate their development and transform their lives.

Making big changes with small steps

Committing to self-development in all aspects of your work, career and your life is the best investment you will ever make. There's genuinely no telling where your commitment to developing yourself could lead. As I reflect on my own career and life, when I intentionally focused on my personal and professional development, I was able to make significant shifts in my performance and potential. The reverse is also true, whenever I've felt busy and overwhelmed, then sacrificed my personal development, I've stalled or even regressed. Making incremental improvements to yourself and your skills every day generates results that are truly exponential.

Reflection is an integral part of the INSPIRe Consultative Sales System – it's fundamental to your improvement, development and success. Invest time in yourself every day, even if it's for just 10 minutes to reflect on your progress. It's worth it. Regardless of the outcome of a patient consultation or team meeting, take time to reflect on how it went and on your performance. Doing so is the simplest and easiest way to dramatically improve your results and stay ahead of your competition.

Here's a simple, fast and effective three-stage reflection practice:

1. Work through self-coaching questions
2. Identify successes and opportunities
3. Commit to improving

Let's walk through these one at a time.

Work through self-coaching questions

High-performing athletes work with a coach, and the same goes for high-performing businesspeople and dental professionals. But if you don't have the luxury of working with a professional coach, you can get into the habit of improving yourself through self-coaching. If you ask yourself these three powerful questions regularly, you'll enhance your performance (I refer to this as the WIN, LEARN, CHANGE model):

1. What are the three key things that went really well? (WIN)
2. What did I learn? (LEARN)
3. What will I change? (CHANGE)

Ask yourself (and answer) these questions at the end of each day, it takes 10-15 minutes maximum.

Identify successes and opportunities

It's important to celebrate your successes. By identifying what has gone well, you create positive momentum for your development. This activity is about becoming consciously aware of and reinforcing what's working for you. Take note of how well you're performing and how much you can improve moving forward. As you reinforce what has gone well, your mind is open to learning more. Through learning, you generate a natural curiosity and greater openness to change. By regularly reflecting and noting the actions you need to take, you can build powerful momentum and your professional development accelerates.

Commit to improving

Finally, commit to maintaining your high performance while also identifying an area that you'll improve upon. This reflection practice is simple and incredibly impactful when repeated regularly. The answers to the questions will create a valuable foundation for your development.

Use this book to guide your development. Revisit the sections and chapters that deliver the most value to you. Consider your development an ongoing process. I like to think of it as committing to lifelong learning. If you choose to, you'll see that there's a lesson in every day, in every interaction and in every person – you just need to look for it. Be open and receptive.

Consultative Sales Mastery: Creative self-coaching

A new perspective

Over time, you may find that your self-coaching 'dries up' and you're struggling to find areas for improvement. The best way to overcome this is to work on your self-coaching creativity. Think about self-assessment in different ways. Below are several self-coaching questions that will help you gain new perspectives:

- What would my mentor (or a leader in this field) recommend I focus on?
- If I were 'the greatest dental professional/ business leader in the world', what would I be doing differently?
- If I had the power of mind control, how would it improve my dentistry?
- What would I do in my patient consultations if I knew I couldn't fail and was guaranteed success?
- If I were capable of anything, what would I do?

Include the answers to these questions in your self-coaching practice to stimulate your creativity and maintain your forward movement and development.

Unlocking your creative self-coaching genius

Within your mind is a genius that can answer any question you ask – you just need to set it free. You're only limited by your imagination. The more you practise asking and answering creative questions, the better you'll get. Here are some more examples of imaginative questions to ask yourself:

- How can I become the best at what I do while creating the most enjoyment for my patient, my team and me?
- What is the most fun I can have in my work?
- Who would I have to become to be the person my patient thinks of before anyone else?
- How can I transform myself and become the most inspirational person my patient and team know?
- What could I do that would make me the happiest dental professional on the planet?
- How could I learn to love my profession and my patients more than anything in the world?
- If I loved what I did so much that it no longer felt like work, what would I have to do?
- What is the most courageous action I could take to inspire my patients and me?
- How could I create so much value for my patients that they felt compelled to show their gratitude forever?

This is only a sample of the questions that you could ask yourself – there is no limit! Taking the opportunity to improve and develop yourself and appreciate and enjoy your patients, your team and your work will set you on a journey that lifts your performance and liberates you. After all, nobody can take away the things you learn and the person you become.

I've developed a self-coaching guide to help you in this journey. You can download a copy of the guide here: https://bit.ly/Reflect-Self-Coach-ICS.

The power of reflection

Self-reflection will stimulate and open up your creative mind. You'll take the time to search for answers and have a strong desire to improve and grow. Once you build a habit of self-reflection, your search for answers will expand beyond developing your dental and/or business talents. If you can harness the power of self-reflection, it will enable continual positive transformation that will impact every part of your life. Self-reflection will become a cornerstone of your development and success in work and life.

Take some time to review your worksheet and make note of the key components of this chapter that you'd like to include in your personalised INSPIRe Consultative Sales System.

Before we move on, reflect on this chapter and write down your thoughts in your journal or notebook.

PART FOUR

LOOKING AHEAD

Chapter 14: Future Success

In 2017 I was the General Sales & Marketing Manager for one of the largest UK business divisions for a multinational corporate. I had developed myself and my skills, taken plenty of risks and opportunities and climbed the career ladder to achieve a position I didn't realise was possible for me. I was leading a team of 48 people and was responsible for a business that was worth over £45 Million pounds each year. I was working in the role I'd pursued for 18 years and was the proud recipient of multiple awards during that time but realised that I really needed a change. I won't go into the details here, but I left the corporate world and wanted to pursue a career, and to do work, that felt more meaningful to me.

Knowing what to do wasn't as easy as it should have been. I worked with a few Executive Coaches during my time there and I really enjoyed and valued the coaching process and results. Working with an experienced Business Coach had always helped me see new perspectives, created clarity, and helped me take more confident decisions and actions. I wanted to give that gift to other business leaders too.

As I mentioned in the introduction of this book, I enrolled in a coaching programme with the Association of Executive Coaching (AoEC) and started on my professional coaching career. The coaching programme was very practical, including the live coaching of real clients throughout.

Combined with my business experience, it was incredibly impactful for the clients I worked with throughout the programme. So much so that all of them became clients thereafter, and most of them are still friends of mine to this day.

When I started working with clients, I found I had attracted a large variation in the types of business, the marketplaces and the sizes of those businesses. I enjoyed the variety and it constantly challenged me with the situations my clients wanted support with. We covered a vast array of topics from, Sales Growth, Coaching Leadership techniques, Facilitation of Board meetings, P&L Management, Team Alignment, Interview processes, Performance Management, and so on. The list of topics my clients were dealing with was enormous and thankfully having had such a varied career in Sales, Business, Leadership and Coaching I could help them navigate these situations with confidence.

Whilst I enjoyed working with a variety of clients, one thing kept playing on my mind: how to create greater relevance and focus on a specific market or type of client. As you'll know from the early chapters of this book, I started my career in dentistry as a dental technician and then spent a further 9 years in dental sales and key account management. I then spent a further 13 years outside of dentistry in Health Care and the IT services sector before returning to work with dental clients in 2018. You would think that focusing on the dental market might be an obvious choice, but I couldn't see it!

I had a number of clients who were in the dental market as suppliers to the profession or larger providers (they include Septodont, the British Dental Industry Association, SDI, Biohorizons and even the MiSmile Network) and yet I still wasn't focusing on the dental market. It wasn't until I was speaking with an entrepreneurs coaching group, I'm part of, and they asked me about my business and in particular "the work and the clients I enjoyed the most". It hit me like a lightning bolt, I really enjoy the dental marketplace. Whilst I'd worked in other markets with other clients, none felt as rewarding or enjoyable as dentistry. It was like coming home.

I made a decision during 2020 that I would reconnect with my dentistry network and reformat my most impactful programmes, content and materials to be tailored towards the dental market and the profession. I've also narrowed my focus to training and coaching on two specialist topics I enjoy and have decades of experience in: 'Consultative Selling' & 'Coaching Leadership'. The opportunity to make this decision was in front of me all the time, for some reason I couldn't see it. Since that decision the clients I work with in the dental marketplace have increased, the programmes I run have been more impactful than ever before and the relationships with people I've met have become even closer. I'm enjoying the work more than I ever have, I'm clearer about the value I offer, and my clients are more appreciative than ever.

You'd be forgiven for thinking, so how does this help me?

Well, here's the point, think about yourself and your practice:

- How clear are you on your areas of special interest?
- How much time, effort and energy have you invested in developing yourself to excel in these areas?
- How well do you communicate this to your patients, your potential patients and your team?
- What is right in front of you or your team, that you just can't see until now?

You may already have the answers to these questions, or you may not, whichever is true for you I encourage you to reflect on them in the coming days, weeks and months. Then combine them with the personal vision we reviewed in Chapter 1. Here it is again:

While there are many different types of visions, two have stood out to me:

- Provide world-class service to my clients or patients
- Be the most trusted and respected supplier to my clients or patients

Imagine if you made it your intention to be both 'world-class' and 'the most trusted and respected provider' to your patients. It will force a new level of thinking about how you operate. When we specialise, we create a new level of relevance for our patients, we improve the quality of our offerings, we develop greater confidence and a superior offering. That makes us stand out from the competition and attracts more of the types of patients we want to treat.

Three Big Ideas

Here are three big ideas for the future of your practice and your career in dentistry:

1 – Think of your practice as a business (if you don't already). Set annual, quarterly & monthly targets for key areas of your business. Consider the following:

- Number of patients per dentist
- Number of Key Treatments (the treatment areas where you have a specialist interest)
- Revenue
- Running Costs
- Profit

2 – Once you have these targets defined, communicate your aspirations with your team. Get them on board so they can help you be accountable and so you have other people aiming for the same targets. Review them with your team regularly to update them of their progress and gain their input into how you can improve performance. You may also want to consider a reward for the team if the targets are met, that way your team is motivated to help you achieve your goals.

3 - Get around the right peer group! If you want to grow and improve yourself, your team and your practice you have to spend time with people who want the same thing. It's said that we become like the 5 people we spend the most time with, be intentional about them. As you surround yourself with higher performers it creates a new level of expectation and helps you embrace the next level. The aim is to 'normalise high performance'. When you do this, you change the trajectory of your performance and future potential.

We've covered a lot of information in this book. The application of what you've learned will give you a massive competitive advantage in your local or national marketplace and in your organisation. What follows is what I consider to be timeless advice. By applying it, along with the content of this book, you'll set yourself on course to be a leader in your field for the life of your career in dentistry.

Embrace Digital, scan every patient

The onset of digital is touching every business, it's becoming an integral part of the value proposition in dentistry. The ability to visualise treatment is a game changer for dentists and patients. Building a library of patient success stories and lives changed is straight forward with the use of an I.O. scanner, digital software and interactive monitor. Many of the dental clients that are growing their private treatments, patients and practices are embracing digital as a way to communicate outcomes to patients. Combine the principles in this book with a digital patient pathway and your growth potential has no limit.

In a client group workshop, I was running the dentists attending discussed their current approach to scanning and one of the most successful practice owners shared her approach. She said, "I scan every patient and have done for the last 12 months". She sent on to explain that since doing soe patient's treatment acceptance has sharply increased, as has the patient's interest in additional treatment options. It's true that a picture paints a thousand words, the scanned image gives the us the chance to truly embrace the principle.

If you haven't done so already, make scanning every patient part of your patient pathway. Incorporate it into every consult and engage the patient in a discussion about their oral health, function and aesthetics. You'll be pleasantly surprised at the results. With the right scanner you also have functionality like 'time-lapse' (as with the iTero scanner from Align Technology). With 'time-lapse' you can clearly show the patient how their teeth are changing over time. It helps you and the track changes and becomes an integral part of your patient records. When comparing treatment provision having a digital practice will become a key deciding factor in future. So my advice is to embrace digital and scan every patient from now on.

Prioritise and execute

As the story at the start of this chapter showed us, not every opportunity is equal. It's critical to your success to identify your greatest strengths, interests, and types of patients. We all have treatments and patients that we know deep down aren't the best use of our time. Be honest with yourself, learn how to better prioritise your time and identify and minimise distractions. Getting clear on where you will invest your time and where you will not be a game-changer.

You need to learn to say no to some patients, colleagues and even your team. Once you're clear on your treatment priorities and the types of patients you want to serve, you must spend a disproportionate amount of time on them. Become laser focused on developing and demonstrating your expertise and maximising your time attracting and serving these patients. The impact this will have on your time and your results might just astound you.

Keep your patient at the heart of everything you do

Let this become your guiding principle in your practice, for yourself and your team. The most important person to you as a dental professional is your patient – the only thing that matters as much is your team. If your patient has an issue, resolve it; if they have a need, you or your team can meet, fulfil it. If you truly have their best interests at heart, they will know it instinctively. You must get this into your unconscious mind. Set your intention to make satisfying your patient your highest priority. Once you've done so, patients will be drawn to be treated by you, your consults will be positive, your network will expand, opportunities will be created effortlessly, and you won't have to concern yourself with patient retention. A genuine focus on creating value for your patients will repay you over and over again. The desire to reciprocate 'value with commitment' is a natural and powerful force in patient–dentist relationships.

Make a promise then over-deliver

I was taught the saying 'over-promise and under-deliver' early in my business career, my own interpretation of it has served me well over the years: 'Make a promise, then over-deliver.' It's not about misleading your patients or misrepresenting the service your practice can deliver – it's about being open, honest and not making promises you can't keep. When you're making commitments to your patients, or they're making requests of you and your practice, you must be honest about what you can and cannot offer. Once you've made a commitment, you must honour it, or you risk damaging your credibility and that of your practice. If possible, create additional value for your patients after a consultation. This is what it means to over-deliver. It's about making an extra effort to delight your patient. It's about giving them something that they didn't expect, which will earn you appreciation and long-term loyalty. This is where the magic happens. Trust in your relationship solidifies and your results accelerate.

Gratitude: give and you shall receive

Whatever your beliefs, I encourage you to cultivate an attitude of gratitude. When you're grateful, everything flows – your relationships get stronger, your outlook on life improves and your confidence grows. Focusing on what you have that you can be grateful for can be a humbling, rewarding practice that gives you a positive perspective on every part of your life. Your patients, colleagues, friends and loved ones will notice and feel even more connected and attracted to you.

If you can combine your attitude of gratitude with a genuine desire to create value for your patients, you'll build healthy, fulfilling relationships based on trust. You'll naturally demonstrate to your patients the confidence and support they need from you to choose you as their preferred partner, a position beyond a dental professional.

Emotions are everything

In Chapter 7, we looked at how emotions are involved in buying decisions. Remember, your patients have a life outside of your consultations. They have friends, family, hobbies, interests and passions. Learn what creates a fire inside your patient, understand what makes their heart sing and find a way to genuinely connect with them in those areas. Being interested in your patient and their life shows your respect and regard for them. Once you've established a common bond, you can build a relationship in which you and your patient make decisions that are best for both of you.

Park your ego

You may work with patients who have an 'edginess' to them. In other words, a sense of superiority and even negativity. In these situations, it can be easy to get drawn into disagreements. You've likely found yourself in consultations where you're desperate to correct your patient or state your opinion after they've said something opinionated or blinkered. Unless you know them very well, or they're not an important patient to you, simply be curious. If you can default to curiosity, you'll bypass your ego. This doesn't mean you should let patients walk all over you – you have values and principles that need to be respected. Rather, you should know when to remain calm and curious. Revisit Chapter 11 and adopt the ritual of 'parking your ego' at the front door when you consult with your patients. It will start to come naturally.

Dentistry and social media

A new world has opened up to dentists and their teams through social media. It's become an influential channel through which you can identify, connect with and influence your patients. Research suggests that as many as 75% of buyers will use social media in their research of suppliers, and the same is true for patients researching treatments. Used consistently and appropriately, social media can enhance and accelerate your credibility with your patients. You can use social media platforms to deliver countless types of content, including the latest trends in dentistry, your practice, your team's and your own accolades, transformational cases, positive patient experiences, case studies and testimonials, all of which will help you attract the attention of your current and future patients. Before you start creating content, cast a critical eye over your social profiles:

- Make sure they're up to date, accurate and professional.
- Ensure they include only relevant and compelling information.
- Check for correct spelling, grammar and capitalisation.
- Identify a connection whose profile looks highly professional and ask for their feedback on your profiles.

This is important because patients will view your profiles before they connect with or follow you. Consider what you want them to think when they view your profiles and make sure they elicit that response. Remember too that patients will be notified of everything you like, comment on and share, so do so considerately and wisely.

Once you're satisfied with your profiles, there are a number of ways in which you can effectively make use of them. Here are some pointers:

Decide on your top three social media objectives and use these as your guide when creating, posting and sharing content. For example:

- Increase my network of potential patients and influencers
- Build credibility and personal brand/ reputation
- Stimulate interest in my content and generate patient enquiries
- Follow experts in your field and comment on and share their content.
- When there's an issue in your marketplace, pose a question about it.
- Use hard data as a reference and/or to raise a challenge.
- Employ humour where possible – consider how your posts can make readers smile.

Pose a question that isn't relevant to your business but is relevant to your patients.

- ➢ Review Facebook Groups and join those that are relevant to your patients and profession.
- ➢ Post images, files and links to interesting sites and content.
- ➢ Create a content plan for social media and invite one of your team to lead it

This list can serve as a starting point. The more engaged you are with social media, the more value you'll get from it.

It's easy to get distracted when using social media, so maintain your discipline when you log in. Develop the habit of logging in for a specific purpose – to meet your three objectives. Capture them in your journal or notebook under the heading Social Media Objectives.

When you use social media to create patient value and generate enquiries, it's no longer a 'social' activity – it's fundamental to your practice growth objectives and you should think about it that way. I encourage you to carefully consider how you can integrate social media into your patient journey and ensure that you or one of your team schedules regular time to act on your recommendations.

A double-edged sword

There are plenty of negative stories about social media out there, and I'm sure you've heard many. It's important to take great care when it comes to your social media profiles and posts. Also, be mindful of where you're being tagged – if your profiles are public, the content linked to you on social media will be visible for all to see. Your profiles act as your shop window to the world, so make sure they're appealing and intentional.

A few years ago, a friend and business acquaintance told me about a role he and a colleague were recruiting for. Prior to interviewing the applicants, they reviewed their profiles on LinkedIn and Facebook to make sure that they matched the branding and image that the company wanted to project. He told me that a search of one applicant's Facebook profile turned up pictures of her dancing topless in a nightclub. She didn't receive an interview. Since hearing this story, I have now made checking LinkedIn and Facebook profiles one of my first tasks when I'm dealing with a new supplier or staff member.

Don't leave it to chance – make sure your profiles are professional.

Ask for testimonials and referrals

We've covered at length the importance of understanding your patients' needs and meeting them. We've looked at how to create value for them. We've agreed that we need to demonstrate trust, confidence and support to satisfy our patients and receive their loyalty and commitment. We've also spoken about asking your patients for feedback at the end of each treatment cycle so you can understand how to better serve them in the future and find ways to continually improve. When you consistently take this approach and genuinely over-deliver it, your patients will want to give you a testimonial and recommend you.

Direct requests for testimonials and recommendations can make some people feel uncomfortable, but there are other ways you can go about it. I suggest asking your most satisfied patients for testimonials and referrals first (prioritise). They'll be your biggest advocates. Whenever you receive a testimonial and/ or referral, show your gratitude. It's the greatest gift a patient can give you. Here are a few ways to generate testimonials and referrals:

- Use your first patient referral as your example and tell other patients how grateful you are for it.

- Create a referral card or leaflet that you can leave with your patients to pass on.
- Include the request for a testimonial early in your patient journey, the earlier you ask people if they will provide a testimonial the more likely they are to do so.
- Write a testimonial script that you can insert into an email. Then ask if your patients would feel comfortable to answer the questions in writing, or video or as a google business review.
- Write a referral script that you can insert into an email. Then ask if your patients would feel comfortable sending it on to people in their network or sharing it on social media.

By integrating patient testimonials and referrals into your patient journey, you'll strengthen your practice brand, expand your patient base and grow your practice more quickly.

Be a lifelong learner

I think of lifelong learning as an attitude towards yourself, your capabilities and, ultimately, your potential in the world. If you acknowledge that you can do anything you set your mind to, and commit to lifelong learning, the path to achieving all of your goals will be laid out for you. There are billions of books in the world. In addition to that, the amount of information available on the internet – tutorials, videos, blogs, webinars, reports, theses, and many, many other mediums – and we have access to almost any type of information we could possibly seek out.

The material is out there. You just need to commit to lifelong learning, decide what you want to study, schedule the right amount (and frequency) of time for it and then apply/practise what you've learned. It really is that simple, but it starts with your commitment.

This is a good time to revisit the goals you set in Chapter 2. Get clear on what you want and work towards it. With commitment and ongoing action, you will create the life you could only have dreamt of in the past. Once you've achieved your goals, you'll no doubt create new, more ambitious ones. Keep surprising yourself in terms of how much you can achieve. And remember to take time to reflect on how far you've come. In the future, when you've achieved your goals and transformed your life, people may ask you how you managed to be so successful. Be generous with your advice and be curious about them – what they want and how you might help.

Identify a mentor

Throughout my career, I've had several informal and formal mentors, all of whom have had a dramatic effect on my career and my life. I've also acted as a mentor to many people within my own and other organisations. It's a truly rewarding experience to support others' growth and help them fulfil their potential. I highly recommend working with a mentor. Here are the steps to take:

- Carefully identify a mentor – someone who has the skills, position, experience or role you aspire to achieve.
- Decide what you want to get from and give to the mentoring relationship.
- Plan how you'll approach your potential mentor.
- Be clear on what you're asking for – the time commitment involved and what their responsibilities are.
- Be humble, grateful, confident and positive when you approach them.

Mentoring is such a positive experience for both parties that, in my experience, it's rare that someone will say no. They may say 'not right now', and that's fine. Ask them when the right time is and schedule the first meeting. Follow the Prepare2 INSPIRe process when preparing for that meeting. You'll then know exactly what you want to get from the meeting and how to be sure of a positive outcome.

If you find the right mentor, you'll have an advocate and adviser for life. This is incredibly beneficial for self-confidence and self-belief. You'll also receive a wealth of personal development from the process of identifying, approaching and planning for the mentoring meetings – and, of course, from the mentoring itself.

Control the temperature

I learned about this quotation and the analogy on a leadership training programme I attended years ago. I love this analogy. It's easy to get swept away by the tide of activity, emotions, relationships and general 'stuff' happening in our lives. We become reactive to our environments, like a thermometer. For example, we may attend meetings where a lot of people complain, including our patients, and end up getting sucked into this attitude and going along with the majority. But you'll know when reacting to the current environment isn't the right thing to do. In these situations, simply ask yourself, 'Do I want to be a thermostat or a thermometer?' Remember, a thermostat sets the temperature. You can create the tone or climate rather than react to it, like a thermometer.

You have the power to choose. Be a thermostat!

Enjoy The Journey

Finally, enjoy your time with patients, your team, friends and family. This might seem like an odd statement in a book like this about business, but the more you enjoy your life, the more your patients will come to like, respect and appreciate you, or even love spending time with you. We spend about half of our waking lives at work – it's half of the journey through life, so it's important to enjoy it.

This enjoyment is a choice, a perspective – it's within your control. You can choose to adopt a sunny disposition and enjoy your current work, or you can choose to move to a role that will bring you this enjoyment.

If you'd like to join the Focus4Growth community, you can connect with us at www.facebook.com/ Focus4growth. You can also join our Facebook group at the following address: www.facebook.com/groups/dentalgrowthleaders

Thank you for reading this book. I wish you the greatest success possible.

I wish you happiness, health and joy.

Most of all, I wish you everything you wish for yourself.

Acknowledgements

Thank you to all the excellent businesspeople I've worked with in the past, the trainers I've had the pleasure of training with and the challenging discussions we've had about what works in practice and what doesn't. Thank you to the best business managers and coaches I've worked with (and the worst) – you can learn something from everyone: the good, the bad and the ugly. Thank you to my many clients and colleagues over the last twenty-eight years, both those who supported me throughout my career and those who challenged me, didn't buy from me and made me reflect, learn, change and drive myself towards continuous improvement.

Thank you to the inspiring authors of the countless books I've had the pleasure of reading – books about dentistry, NLP, psychology, success, business leadership, sales, coaching and performance. The application of this information has shaped and strengthened me throughout my career and my life, and thankfully the journey continues!

Thank you to my family for your never-ending belief in my abilities, my journey and the future destination. I know I've challenged the boundaries with my ideas, creativity and future vision, but what is life for if not to dream big?

The Author

Justin Leigh is the founder and managing director of Focus-4Growth Ltd, a Sales & Leadership Training Company specialising in the dental market. He's the best-selling author of INSPIRE, INFLUENCE, SELL and works with market-leading Dental Companies like Align Technology, W&H, Septodont, BioHorizons and many more. In 2020 he was invited to become the Sales Training Partner for the British Dental Industry Association.

A business owner with over twenty-eight years' experience in sales, strategic account management and business leadership, he has a track record of rapidly growing businesses across multiple market segments. An accredited executive coach, Justin is also an accomplished author, trainer, facilitator, adviser and consultant to board-level executives and teams.

Justin is passionate about helping people to grow, inspiring them to reach outstanding levels of performance through continuous improvement and clear, accountable action.

He is the author of a number of sales and business growth programmes, including:

- Inspire Consult, Sell – Dental Professionals Consultative Sales Training Programme
- Inspire, Influence, Sell - Sales Training Programme
- The Connect, Contract Coach – Coaching Leadership Programme

- Increasing Resilience and Accelerating Productivity Programmes
- The Leadership Acceleration Programme

Justin and the Focus4growth team's mission is to bring world class business best practice to our clients and show them how they can become market leaders in their field.

Justin lives in Cambridgeshire, England, with his wife and two children.

Contact

If you would like to enquire about working with Justin and his team at Focus4Growth, you can connect and contact him at:

https://linktr.ee/JustinLeigh

LinkedIn: www.linkedin.com/in/business-sales-acceleration

Facebook: www.facebook.com/justin.leigh.71/about

www.facebook.com/groups/dentalgrowthleaders

Website: www.focus4growth.co.uk

Instagram: @focus4growth
Tik Tok: @oneminutecoach

SCAN ME